KT-453-878

The Critically Reflective Practitioner

Sue Thompson
Neil Thompson

610.7301 THO

LIS LIBRARY

Date	Fund
25/6/12	U-che.

Order No
2313832 .

University of Chester

© Sue Thompson and Neil Thompson 2008

All rights reserved. No reproduction, copy or transmission of this publication may be made without written permission.

No portion of this publication may be reproduced, copied or transmitted save with written permission or in accordance with the provisions of the Copyright, Designs and Patents Act 1988, or under the terms of any licence permitting limited copying issued by the Copyright Licensing Agency, Saffron House, 6-10 Kirby Street, London EC1N 8TS.

Any person who does any unauthorized act in relation to this publication may be liable to criminal prosecution and civil claims for damages.

The authors have asserted their rights to be identified as the authors of this work in accordance with the Copyright, Designs and Patents Act 1988.

First published 2008 by
PALGRAVE MACMILLAN

Palgrave Macmillan in the UK is an imprint of Macmillan Publishers Limited, registered in England, company number 785998, of Houndmills, Basingstoke, Hampshire RG21 6XS.

Palgrave Macmillan in the US is a division of St Martin's Press LLC, 175 Fifth Avenue, New York, NY 10010.

Palgrave Macmillan is the global academic imprint of the above companies and has companies and representatives throughout the world.

Palgrave® and Macmillan® are registered trademarks in the United States, the United Kingdom, Europe and other countries.

ISBN-13: 978–0–230–57318–5
ISBN-10: 0–230–57318–5

This book is printed on paper suitable for recycling and made from fully managed and sustained forest sources. Logging, pulping and manufacturing processes are expected to conform to the environmental regulations of the country of origin.

A catalogue record for this book is available from the British Library.

A catalog record for this book is available from the Library of Congress.

10 9 8 7 6 5
17 16 15 14 13 12 11

Printed in China

For John

Contents

Preface

Reflective practice is not a new idea, but it is one that has seen a massive growth of interest in recent years. Increasingly, people engaged in education and training programmes are being encouraged, if not actually required, to be reflective. And, to a lesser extent, it is now being recognized that reflective practice should be seen as a foundation for all professional practice – that is, not simply something that is carried out as part of gaining a qualification or professional award. However, it is unfortunately the case that the growth of interest has not been matched by an equivalent growth in understanding. We have found that many people have but a superficial understanding of reflective practice, what it means, how it can or should be used or why it is important.

What we have also found (for example, through running training courses on reflective practice) is that once people have a better understanding of the subject and how useful it can be for their work, they develop a strong commitment to making reflective practice a reality and are keen to find out more about what is involved. This book is intended, then, as a platform from which interested readers can (i) establish a good understanding of the nature and usefulness of reflective practice; and (ii) explore how to make such practice a reality.

This is a *practical* book, but, in keeping with the philosophy underpinning reflective practice, the practice we are advocating needs to be *informed* practice. That is, it is not a case of emphasizing practice *as opposed to* theory, but rather of promoting good practice *through* theory. In other words, this is a book that recognizes the importance of actual practice, but which also recognizes the need for such practice to be based on professional knowledge and values. Indeed, this is at the heart of reflective practice – making sure that the work that we do is informed by a knowledge base that is open to scrutiny and challenge (and is therefore not dogmatic) and a clear value base that is consistent with our professional duties. It is recognized that it is dangerous to allow our practice to be based on habit, routine, mindless following of procedures, simply copying what others do and an unclear value base that may at times run counter to our professional aims.

Reflective practice can be effective, rewarding and ethical practice that makes a positive contribution to continuous professional development and to promoting improvements in professional practice. Non-reflective practice, by contrast, can be ineffective, demotivating (if not soul destroying) and unethical practice that discourages learning and development and reinforces low standards of professional practice. This book is intended as a guide to making sure, as far as we reasonably can, that our professional efforts contribute more to the former than to the latter.

The authors have a background in nursing, social work, education and management – and these are all areas in which reflective practice has an important contribution to make. However, what we have to say in the book will be of value across the helping professions, including other aspects of health and social care; youth and community work; probation and youth justice work; counselling and psychotherapy; advice, guidance and pastoral work; and related occupations.

For students and practitioners, the book should offer a helpful contribution to developing your understanding and thus your practice. For managers, supervisors, mentors, coaches and practice teachers, there is an additional layer of learning that the book offers, in so far as there is much within its pages that will be of value in terms of not only developing your own practice, but also that of the people you are supporting in their learning. That is, the insights offered in the book will be helpful at two levels: developing our own reflective practice and supporting others (students, supervisees and so on) in developing their reflective practice.

This book will not provide magic answers, but what it will do is provide a clear foundation of understanding and a basis for developing your knowledge and skills over time. We anticipate that it will be a text that you will find helpful to read from cover to cover to begin with, but then to have as a reference source and reminder thereafter. We very much hope you will find it of benefit in maximizing your potential not only for learning, but also for high-quality professional practice that makes a real difference to the lives of the people we serve.

Acknowledgements

We have had the assistance of a number of people in producing this book. Catherine Gray and Sheree Keep at the publishers have once again been very helpful in supporting us through the process. Dr Sharon Brimfield-Edwards of Avenue Consulting Ltd was a sterling researcher on our behalf and Anna Thompson, also of Avenue Consulting Ltd, played an important practical role in various ways. We are also grateful to Penny Simmons for her high-quality copyediting work.

We have had the benefit of helpful comments from a number of esteemed colleagues who have been kind enough to review an earlier draft of the book. We therefore owe a debt of thanks to John Bates and Pat Brignall of Liverpool Hope University, Professor Bernard Moss of Staffordshire University and Graham Thompson of Bangor University.

The book is dedicated to our colleague and long-time friend, John Bates. The dedication is in large part a recognition of his solid friendship over the years and how much we appreciate it. It is also a recognition of his contribution over the years to developing critically reflective approaches as a foundation for professional education and practice in the helping professions.

Introduction

There is already a significant literature on the subject of reflective practice (see the *Guide to Further Learning* at the end of the book). This book is not intended to be simply another one to add to the list. Rather, our aim is to provide a basic introduction to the theory and practice involved in a reflective approach that will also act as a gateway to the wider literature base and the insights it offers.

The book is divided into two main parts. Part 1 focuses mainly on the theory base underpinning reflective practice in general and critically reflective practice in particular, outlining some of the key issues that combine to give us what we will refer to as a philosophy of reflective practice – a set of concepts that provide a framework of understanding and a foundation for our practice. Part 2 focuses mainly on the practice base, in the sense that it is here that we explore ways and means of promoting reflective practice. Each part is divided into three chapters, and these are supplemented by a concluding chapter that draws out, under the heading of 'rising to the challenge', the steps we need to take to make reflective practice a reality.

Chapter 1 examines the nature of reflective practice. This involves identifying some myths and misunderstandings relating to reflective practice. This is an important contribution to our understanding, as superficial and misleading conceptions of reflective practice are unfortunately not uncommon phenomena. This chapter also traces ideas of reflective practice back to the seminal work of Donald Schön and, in doing so, establishes a degree of clarity about what is actually meant by reflective practice. In addition, the importance of integrating theory and practice is examined, and the nature and importance of professional knowledge are discussed. Finally, this chapter explores what is involved in critical reflection and thus in *critically* reflective practice.

Chapter 2 is concerned with three different (but related) dimensions of reflective practice. First, we consider the cognitive dimension – that is, the ways in which thinking, particularly critical thinking, is a vitally important underpinning of reflective practice. Second, we emphasize that, despite some common misconceptions of reflective practice, it is not simply a matter of thinking about what we do – there is also a highly important emotional dimension. Staff and managers in the helping professions who have only a limited understanding of how emotions feature in people's lives in general, and the world of professional practice in particular, run the risk of doing more harm than good. This chapter shows that reflective practice needs to be emotionally sensitive practice. Third, the significance of values is emphasized – reflecting on values is also part of the process.

The subject matter of Chapter 3 is the contextual basis of reflection. It is concerned with how reflection needs to take place at three different levels: individual; one to one; and group. First, we look at what is referred to as 'personal reflective space', which involves establishing how we can develop the working habits and systems we need to promote our own reflective practice. Second, we explore how one-to-one sessions (supervision, mentoring or coaching) can be an important part of developing reflective approaches to our work. Third, we map out how group approaches to reflection and learning can also be an important part of the equation. Overall, this chapter paints a picture of how reflective practice needs to be understood as more than just an individual, solitary activity.

Chapter 4 is the first chapter in Part 2. In it our focus is on strategies and techniques that can be usefully deployed to help us work in a reflective way. In other words, we identify a range of 'tools' that can be used to good effect to promote reflective practice. What is offered is not a definitive or exhaustive list, but should be sufficient to establish how such techniques and frameworks can provide a platform for informed approaches to practice. This chapter offers useful suggestions that apply at two levels: developing our own practice and playing a supportive or facilitative role in promoting other people's reflective practice. It shows how a knowledge of such strategies and techniques can be a valuable basis for drawing on the advantages offered by a well-informed reflective approach.

Chapter 5 examines two related sets of issues. First, it helps us to understand the relationship between reflective thinking and reflective writing – both important components of critically reflective practice. Based on the idea that accounts of practice are an excellent way of both demonstrating evidence of reflection (as part of a portfolio for an educational award, for example) and providing a foundation for learning (through a reflective log or diary, for example), the first part of Chapter 5 offers guidance on effective approaches to reflective writing. Second, it highlights what is involved in assessing reflective accounts when, for example, assessors are called upon to form a judgement on the quality of written work produced as part of an educational programme. The basic message of the chapter is that genuinely reflective writing can be a useful aid to clarifying our thinking and thus our practice.

In Chapter 6 we identify a range of obstacles that can stand in the way of reflective practice. Some of these relate to themes and issues mentioned earlier in the book, while others are introduced here for the first time. An important point arising from this chapter is that there *will* be barriers, there *will* be things that make reflection difficult or otherwise discourage us, but we do not have to allow these to defeat us – there are ways and means of overcoming, removing or avoiding these obstacles, or at least of minimizing their impact. An important part of this is working together to develop a culture of reflection and learning. The more successful we are in this, the easier it will be to tackle the obstacles that stand in our way.

As we noted earlier, Chapter 7 is the concluding chapter that sums up the main steps we need to take to put reflective practice firmly on the agenda within our own career paths and more broadly within our employing organizations and professional arenas.

Overall, the book provides a theoretically informed practical guide rooted in many years' experience of professional practice, management and education on the part of the authors. As such, it mirrors the philosophy of reflective practice: blending knowledge, experience and practice in ways that are productive and constructive as a foundation for helping others and for developing our capabilities to the maximum.

Part 1

Understanding Reflective Practice

Chapter 1

What is Reflective Practice?

INTRODUCTION

When good ideas become very popular, there is a danger that they also become oversimplified and used in a superficial way, thereby failing to do justice to the complexities involved. And there are lots of complexities involved. This is partly because reflective practice has grown up in different professional disciplines and contexts, each with their own subtle differences and nuances. As Moon (1999) comments:

> The work on reflection in the context of practice – reflective practice – originated mainly in the professions of teaching and nursing, but there is little integration of these two sources, and relatively few professional educators have crossed boundaries, even if they have been attempting to develop similar attributes in their novices or their trained professionals. It is as if reflection has been viewed through a series of narrow frames of reference, with little overlap.
>
> (pp. vii–viii)

To this we can add a significant body of literature relating to reflective practice in social work and a growing literature on how reflective practice can also be seen to apply in a management context. Our aim here, though, is not to explore these differences, but rather to focus on the commonalities: what are the key concepts and themes that help us make sense of reflective practice and the philosophy underpinning it?

However, before examining what is now commonly understood as reflective practice, we first want to clear up some widespread misunderstandings. This will clear the way for developing a more sophisticated understanding of our subject matter and its importance across the various disciplines within the helping professions. Such misunderstandings are both a reflection of the common tendency to adopt an oversimplified and superficial approach to reflective practice and, in large part, a major contributor to the persistence of that unhelpful and dangerously superficial approach.

We begin our discussion of the nature of reflective practice, then, by identifying common misunderstandings and thus, in effect, commenting on what reflective practice is *not*, before establishing what it actually is.

WHAT REFLECTIVE PRACTICE IS NOT

We have encountered a number of misunderstandings over the years about the nature and role of reflective practice, some relatively minor, some quite seriously adrift from what reflective practice is actually all about. We shall focus here on the major discrepancies and identify why each one of them is problematic.

A luxury we can't afford

A common initial reaction to reflective practice when people are introduced to it for the first time is to express the view that it is a good idea in principle, but not really workable in practice due to the pressures of work – it is seen as 'a luxury we can't afford'. This is an understandable response, albeit a mistaken and misleading one. While it is certainly true that levels of work pressure can be very high, perhaps too high on many occasions if the incidence of stress is anything to go by, this does not rule out reflective practice. This is because a key underlying principle of reflective practice is that the busier we are, the more reflective we need to be. That is, the more under pressure we are, the more each of us needs to be thinking clearly and carefully about:

■   What are my roles and duties? Am I clear about what is expected of me?

- What are my goals? How will I be able to achieve them?
- What are my priorities? What is the best use of my time?
- What strategies are available to me in order to manage the pressures I face?
- Who can I rely upon to support me? Who can I collaborate with?
- What previous learning can I draw upon to help me cope with my current challenges?

Making the time and finding the space in our minds to do this can be quite a challenge at times, but it is none the less worth the effort to do so, as having what learning and development expert David Clutterbuck calls 'reflective space' is a fundamental ingredient of high-quality practice:

> Although people are often working longer hours than a decade ago, they have less and less time to stop and think deeply. In experiments with hundreds of managers and professionals, less than 3 per cent claim to find their deep thinking time at work, and of these, the majority do so by coming in very early in the morning. For most people, however, deep thinking time happens on the journey to and from work, in the bath, or shower, taking exercise, doing the ironing, lying awake at night, or in other parts of their 'free' time.
>
> Deep, reflective thinking is as essential to the effectiveness of our conscious brain as REM sleep is to our unconscious. In both cases, we become dysfunctional if our minds do not carry out the essential task of analysing, structuring, organising and storing. When we allow ourselves to enter *personal reflective space* (PRS), we put the world around us largely on hold.
>
> (Clutterbuck, 2001, pp. 21–3)

We shall return to the idea of 'personal reflective space' in Chapter 3. However, for now, we can agree with Clutterbuck that there can be difficulties involved in creating reflective space, but also note that the efforts needed are an important investment of our time and energy.

The discussions in this and subsequent chapters should help in this regard by emphasizing the importance of making time and space for reflective practice and the dangers of not doing so.

Practice focus 1.1

Elaine came home from work each day feeling exhausted. What made it worse was that she found it difficult to relax at evenings and weekends as she felt under so much pressure at work. She had so little time to think that she felt her work was out of control – and that made her feel very uncomfortable indeed. However, all this was to change when she attended a course on reflective practice and was introduced to the principle that the busier we are, the more reflective we need to be. After this she made sure that she focused very carefully on her work pressures, making sure that she stopped to think and plan. She recognized that she had become so busy that she had 'lost the plot' in relation to many aspects of her work. By being more thoughtful about her work, she was able to avoid the feelings of helplessness that had slowed her down, demoralized her and led her to waste a lot of time. She found it quite a struggle at first to adopt this new way of working, but after a while she felt much more comfortable and in control. Her morale rose, she made fewer mistakes and she was able to get much more done in the time available. Even though her work schedule was still tough and demanding, she realized that this more reflective approach paid dividends. She was still tired each day when she went home but, as she was more in control of her work, she was quickly able to relax and enjoy her time off.

A magical process

A significant part of the oversimplified, superficial approach to reflective practice mentioned above is the assumption that reflective practice is simply a matter of pausing for thought from time to time. It is mistakenly assumed that engaging in practice, then stopping to reflect on that practice, practising some more and then reflecting some more will somehow produce learning and higher standards of practice – as if by magic. Of course, the reality is much more complex than this. Reflective practice does involve a degree of reflecting on our practice, but in specific ways and as part of a broader process – and not simply a process of pausing for thought.

Learning will not take place and practice will not develop if no connections are made between the thinking and the doing. That is, if we are not able to understand what we are doing and why we are doing it as part of a broader, more holistic picture of our work, the goals we are pursuing and how we are pursuing them. When we look more closely below at what is actually involved in reflective practice, we will be able to see more clearly how simplistic and inadequate this 'magical' perspective on reflection is.

A solitary pursuit

Most of the literature relating to reflective practice paints a picture of individual practitioners ploughing their own furrow in terms of developing reflective approaches to their practice. There has been comparatively less analysis or discussion of how people can support one another in shared endeavour or how organizations can support their staff and managers in their efforts – for example, by promoting reflective workplace cultures and making informed and considered practice a standard expectation rather than something only a minority can be expected to achieve. However, while the main focus clearly is on individual practitioners, there is none the less a significant and growing literature on, and understanding of, the wider social and organizational aspects of reflective practice (see, for example, Gould and Baldwin, 2004; Thompson, 2006a).

It would indeed be a mistake to adopt too individualistic an approach to reflection. Reflective practice need not be a solitary activity. As we shall see in Chapter 3, there is much to be gained from people working together towards shared aims of reflective practice and the benefits it brings, and from organizations taking seriously their responsibilities towards maximizing learning and, in the process, maximizing quality of practice. It needs to be remembered that the 'practice' we are referring to in the term 'reflective practice' includes management practice. That is, we see it as important for managers to make their practice reflective too. This not only makes for better management (in terms of informed decision making, for example), but also for a more fertile environment for reflective practice across the whole organization.

Limited to education and training programmes

A very common misunderstanding is that reflective practice is intended to be specifically a feature of education or training programmes, rather than a feature of good practice more generally. We have encountered many people who have been surprised that we have an expectation that reflective practice should be adopted as an overall aspect of our work, rather than something restricted to gaining a qualification or professional award.

This perception of reflective practice as a limited undertaking can combine with the earlier misapprehension that 'we are too busy to be reflective'. That is, it is assumed that it is worth the effort to be reflective as part of a programme of studies, but too demanding to be part of everyday practice. Again, this fails to appreciate how reflective practice can, and should, be seen as an *investment* of time, not a time cost. A continuous commitment to reflective practice means not only that we get the benefits of reflection on an ongoing basis, but also that we can develop our knowledge, skills and confidence in reflective practice over time – that is, we can become more expert in the use of reflective techniques and thus get even more value from the efforts we invest.

An alternative to theory

A significant element of reflective practice is the process of drawing out learning from our experience, to be able to distil useful learning points that will guide our future practice from our current or recent practice activities. While this certainly is a key part of the process, it can be misleading to see it in isolation by not taking account of the wider context of which this forms only one part. Without this wider understanding it is easy for people to make the mistaken assumption that reflective practice is an alternative to drawing on theory. If the traditional approach can be characterized as applying theory to practice, then the reflective approach can be seen, according to this mistaken view, as applying practice to practice – that is, drawing out our learning from our practice experiences without reference to theory, research or professional knowledge more broadly.

Such a narrow, oversimplified approach fails to take account of the important role of professional knowledge in shaping practice. Even though we may often not be directly aware of the role of such knowledge in influencing our practice, it would be a significant mistake not to acknowledge the major part it plays. Unless we consciously think about (that is, reflect on) the role of theory, we are likely to fail to see the invisible hand of our knowledge base shaping our assumptions and understandings. But it would be a far-reaching error to confuse 'invisible' with 'absent'. At the heart of reflective practice is the process of becoming aware of the knowledge that informs our practice – making it more visible. This is a point to which we shall return below under the heading of 'Drawing on knowledge'. However, for now, it is important to note that drawing out the learning from experience should not be confused with the mistaken notion that theoretical concerns are not relevant to practice or indeed to learning.

Displaced by evidence-based practice

In recent years we have seen the growth of another very influential approach to professional practice, namely evidence-based practice. The basis of this approach is that practice should be informed by the best evidence available, particularly research evidence – for example, the results of 'random controlled clinical trials' (where some people are given a placebo instead of the actual 'treatment' so that it can be established whether the treatment actually works). Unfortunately, some people have made the mistake of assuming that the rise of evidence-based practice makes reflective practice unnecessary – as if to assume that we no longer need to reflect on practice, we simply have to do what the research evidence indicates to be the best way forward.

This shows a significant misunderstanding of both research evidence (and how it can be used) and reflective practice. Research evidence in the helping professions will often not be clear cut in terms of giving precise guidance for practice. While research can, and often does, cast light on practice issues, it is rarely the case that the research is so definitive that it gives us a clear path to follow. Even if it did, we would still need reflective practice in order to be able to integrate those research findings into our wider knowledge base and experience so that they can be of use to us. Research, like the professional knowledge base more broadly, is not something that we should follow slavishly or uncritically, as such an approach would leave us very ill-equipped to deal with the complex demands of working with people and their problems across the helping professions.

THE LEGACY OF SCHÖN

Having considered some misconceptions about reflective practice, it is now time for us to look at what is really meant by the term. To do that we shall look initially at the work of one of the most influential thinkers in relation to reflective practice, namely Donald Schön. He was not the first person to explore reflective practice (for example, Dewey was writing about such issues in the first quarter of the twentieth century – Dewey, 1916; 1933), but his work has played a major role in bringing the subject to the attention of a wide range of professionals and professional educators.

Schön was an educationalist with an interest in how professionals across various disciplines develop their respective knowledge bases and actually use them in practice. He was aware that it is not simply a matter of drawing on one's knowledge base in a direct or simple way. That is, he realized that a professional knowledge base rarely, if ever, gives direct practice guidance on what to do and how to do it. For example, a knowledge of the law does not tell a member of the legal profession how to practise law, just as a knowledge of the human body, disease processes and so on does not give health care professionals a set of instructions about how to undertake their duties. If there is no direct relationship between professional knowledge (that is, the theory and research base) and practice, what is the nature of the relationship? This was Schön's field of study; this is what he wanted to make sense of. And it was the notion of reflective practice that he developed to do this.

The critique of technical rationality

The idea that theory, or knowledge more broadly, can be applied directly to practice goes under the heading of 'technical rationality'. Schön was very critical of this approach as he felt it was far from adequate for explaining the complexities involved:

> Technical Rationality is the Positivist epistemology of practice. It became institutionalized in the modern university, founded in the late nineteenth century when Positivism was at its height, and in the professional schools which secured their place in the university in the early decades of the twentieth century.
>
> (1983, p. 31)

Positivism is an approach to the social sciences that naively assumes that human affairs can be understood in terms of scientific laws, in the same way that the natural sciences understand the physical world in terms of laws of nature. Such an approach fails to do justice to the complexity, diversity and variability of human life (see Thompson, 2000, for a discussion of this). Technical rationality is therefore an approach to professional practice that involves trying to establish fixed ways of working, established 'right answers' for how to proceed. Schön was able to see that this did not fit with the reality of professional practice, what he referred to as the 'swampy lowlands' of practice – a terrain that is messy, difficult and confusing.

Rolfe, Freshwater and Jasper share Schön's mistrust of technical rationality when they comment that:

> We can see that, if followed rigidly, the technical rationality model reduces practitioners to the level of technicians whose only role is to implement the research findings and theoretical models of the scientists, researchers and theoreticians.
>
> (2001, p. 7)

It is significant to note that, despite the clear limitations of positivist attempts to apply natural science methodology to the social sciences in general and social work in particular, this approach has manifested itself in some aspects of what has come to be known as evidence-based practice (see the *Guide to Further Learning* for further information about this). It is also fair to say that, while the growth of interest in reflective practice has contributed significantly to the rejection of technical rationality and its underlying positivism, there are still clear elements of this form of rigid rationality apparent across the helping professions and their associated professional educational systems.

As an alternative to this unsatisfactory model of professional practice, Schön preferred to see the professional knowledge base not as a 'scientific' source of 'right answers', but rather as the cloth from which practitioners tailor their professional response. That is, we cannot expect professional knowledge to provide 'off-the-peg' solutions, like a garment in a clothes shop. Rather, it is a matter of the knowledge base serving as a resource (a set of insights and understandings) that needs to be adapted to suit the circumstances. In other words, the reflective practitioner acts as a skilled tailor, using the knowledge base of his or her profession as the cloth from which to cut appropriate solutions to fit the requirements of the specific practice situation. This introduces the notion of professional 'artistry'. Schön recognized there is a scientific knowledge base (part natural science, part social science) that can be drawn upon, but also realized that a degree of artistry is needed to make meaningful links between that knowledge base (what Schön referred to as the 'high ground' that gives us an overview of the terrain below) and the actual demands of practice (the 'swampy lowlands').

Reflection and action

A key part of Schön's work is his distinction between reflection-in-action and reflection-on-action. The former refers to the thinking we do while actually practising, a sort of 'thinking on our feet'. For example, we may be listening carefully to what someone is telling us and trying to relate that to our specific role in that situation, the problem we are trying to address and so on. In doing so we will be drawing on not only our previous experience, but also our professional knowledge base (see the discussion of 'Drawing on knowledge' below). The latter refers to reflection after the event – that is, where we later review our experience, make sense of it, try to learn from it and so on.

Ideally, reflection-in-action and reflection-on-action should interconnect. That is, our reflection-on-action should refer back to what was going through our mind during the actual practice encounter (reflection-in-action 1), while the next time we are engaged in such practice, our reflection (reflection-in-action 2) should draw on our previous reflection-on-action. This then sets up a cycle in which we integrate the two sets of reflection and thus provide a basis for 'cutting our cloth'. In this way we are able to facilitate the integration of theory and practice – that is, to make sure practice is informed by theory and theory is informed (and tested) by practice. We shall return to this important topic below.

One aspect of the relationship between reflection and action that Schön does not discuss is what we shall refer to as 'reflection-for-action'. This refers to planning, being able to think ahead about what we might encounter – for example, to try and anticipate what is likely to happen, what we need to do, what we may need to be wary of (a risk of aggression or violence, for example) and so on. Reflection-on-action can therefore not only refer back to the earlier reflection-*in*-action, but also look forward in terms of reflection-*for*-action. This is an important point in relation to our earlier discussion of making time for reflection. Being able to anticipate difficulties and generally plan ahead can make for a very effective use of time. It can also give us a greater sense of control and confidence that will tend to have a positive effect on our morale and motivation – and thereby enable us to achieve more in the limited time available.

Benner, Hooper-Kyriakidis and Stannard write of the importance of fore-thought:

> The most effective clinical forethought is based both on scientific understanding and experiential learning of clinical trajectories. Clinical forethought does not have to be precisely correct to be a useful basis for thinking-in-action; it only needs to be in the right direction or region of the problem and capable of being confirmed or discon-firmed by the actual evolving situation. Clinical forethought works best when it is held tentatively and when it flexibly changes if the patient's condition unfolds in an unexpected direction. Rigid adher-ence to what one has anticipated and planned for is a source of error in this habit of thought because it prevents seeing the unexpected.
> (1999, p. 65)

What this passage captures is the important point that, while planning or fore-thought is an important aspect of professional practice, it should not become a rigid adherence to a fixed way of working. As we shall see below, flexibility and creativity are important parts of reflective practice.

The organizational context

Schön's work has proved extremely influential over an extended period of time. It is generally characterized by an emphasis on the individual, with rela-tively little attention paid to the wider context. However, Schön does make reference to the importance of the organizational context of practice:

> When a member of a bureaucracy embarks on a course of reflec-tive practice, allowing himself to experience confusion and uncer-tainty, subjecting his frames and theories to conscious criticism and change, he may increase his capacity to contribute to significant organizational learning, but he also becomes, by the same token, a danger to the stable system of rules and procedures within which he is expected to deliver his technical expertise.

> Thus ordinary bureaucracies tend to resist a professional's attempt to move from technical expertise to reflective practice. And conversely, an organization suited to reflective practice would have features very different from those of familiar bureaucratic settings.
>
> (1983, pp. 328–9)

What this tells us is that the organizational context is an important factor (or set of factors) when it comes to developing reflective practice. As we shall see below, this means that promoting reflective practice will often involve seeking to influence the culture of the organization in which we work in an attempt to make it more receptive to, and supportive of, reflective practice.

Voice of experience 1.1

When I moved to my current job I thought I was on a different planet rather than just in a different organization. Where I worked before, the emphasis was on simply getting the job done. Raising standards of practice, being able to learn and grow in the job or going for the best quality we could were just not on the agenda at all. I am just so delighted to be in a place now where we are encouraged to reflect on what we are doing and work towards optimal outcomes, not just achieving the bare minimum. It is just so refreshing, and morale here is so much higher. In my old job I always felt I didn't have time to be more reflective, but the culture and atmosphere here are so much more positive that we actually get much more done in the time available. It's amazing; so much better.

Stuart, a youth justice worker

Strengths and weaknesses of Schön's approach

The major strengths of Schön's work include the following:

- It offers a helpful understanding of the relationship between professional knowledge and professional practice, recognizing that both theory and practice have an important contribution to make to learning and development.
- It helps us move away from unhelpful, simplistic approaches based on the idea of 'technical rationality'.

■ It provides a platform for continuous learning and optimal outcomes as a result of enhanced standards of practice.

However, there are also weaknesses or areas for development that can be identified, not least the following:

■ There is a predominant (but not exclusive) emphasis on the individual, therefore wider social and organizational factors are not given sufficient attention.
■ It pays insufficient attention to the need for *critical* reflection (see below) and an understanding of the key role of power relations.
■ It focuses on the rational aspects of reflection and practice and thereby neglects the emotional dimension of such matters.

These limitations will be addressed to a limited extent in the pages that follow, but it is beyond the scope of this book to develop a comprehensive evaluation of Schön's work. For present purposes, our comments here should be sufficient to make it clear that Schön's work has proved to be a very positive contribution to our understanding, but still leaves many areas in need of further development.

Reflective or reflexive?

Schön and most of his followers consistently use the term 'reflective'. However, many writers have adopted a similar, but significantly different term, namely 'reflexive'. We should not allow their similarity to confuse us into thinking they are the same or interchangeable. They are related ideas, but there are also key differences. What, then, is meant by these two terms?

'Reflective' is an ambiguous term. It is generally used to refer to reflection in the sense of thinking, as in: 'I'm not sure about that; let me reflect on it for a moment'. However, it can also be used in the sense of reflecting in the way a mirror does. Reflective, in this sense, means looking back on ourselves – in effect, being self-aware. Both senses of reflective are therefore very relevant to our usage of the term 'reflective practice': it involves both thinking/analysis and self-awareness.

'Reflexive' is a term that largely overlaps with this second sense of reflective. Fook and Askeland clarify the idea of reflexivity:

> Reflexivity can simply be defined as an ability to recognize our own influence – and the influence of our social and cultural contexts on research, the type of knowledge we create, and the way we create it (Fook 1999b). In this sense, then, it is about factoring ourselves as players into the situations we practice in.
>
> (2006, p. 45)

Rolfe, Freshwater and Jasper (2001), in discussing reflective practice in nursing, relate this to Schön's distinction between reflection-in-action and reflection-on-action: 'Thus, if the nurse who reflects on action is a *reflective* practitioner, then the one who reflects in action is a *reflexive* practitioner' (p. 129). By this they appear to mean that reflection-in-action is reflexive (self-aware, tuned into our own role and influence in the process), while reflection-on-action is reflective (in the sense of 'thoughtful'). However, we would not see it this way. Our view is that reflection-in-action and reflection-on-action need to be both thoughtful and self-aware. We therefore understand reflexive practice to be a dimension of reflective practice. In our view, reflective practice needs to be reflective in both senses of the word: thoughtful (analytical and well-informed) as well as self-aware or 'reflexive'.

INTEGRATING THEORY AND PRACTICE

Traditional approaches to the relationship between theory and practice have tended to portray it as a one-way street – that is, as a process in which theoretical knowledge is applied to practice. We begin with theory and work towards practice. However, reflective practice is based on a different understanding of the relationship between the two, one in which theory and practice are given equal billing – that is, where there is a two-way relationship in which the knowledge base and the practice base are interconnected, neither having more importance than the other. As has been recognized for some years now, theory without practice is of little use and practice without theory can be very dangerous. We therefore need to give closer attention to the relationship between theory and practice, between knowing and doing.

Our concern is with *integrating* theory and practice – that is, with showing how theory underpins practice and practice informs theory (in the sense that accounts of practice can help to test and develop theory over time).

Practice focus 1.2

Ravinder's professional training had taught her that people grieve in stages. However, after a few months in her new job working with people who had experienced a major loss, she became very suspicious about what she had learned. She could see little evidence of people grieving in stages. To her it was more a case of grief being a 'roller-coaster' ride, going up and down, round and round – quite violently sometimes. As a result of this, she started to read up on contemporary theories of grief. She quickly discovered that simple stage theories had been superseded by more sophisticated understandings of loss. She began to realize that these theories were far more consistent with what she had been witnessing in practice. She recognized that the traditional theory had been quite influential, and yet ironically the more up-to-date theory was more in tune with what was happening in practice. This experience made her aware that there were dangers involved in relying on theory – however well established it might be – that has not been tested in practice. She began to appreciate that the relationship between theory and practice was much more complex than she had initially thought.

In terms of this relationship, Schön makes an interesting point when he states that:

> I have become convinced that universities are not devoted to the production and distribution of fundamental knowledge in general. They are institutions committed, for the most part, to a particular epistemology, a view of knowledge that fosters selective inattention to practical competence and professional artistry.
>
> (1983, p. vii)

By this we understand him to mean that he is aware of the need to develop a much clearer focus on (i) how knowledge can inform practice ('practical competence'); and (ii) the skills involved in using such knowledge in practice ('professional artistry'). A quarter of a century after Schön wrote this, we can see that there is now a much closer concentration on the use of knowledge in practice and that the focus on reflective practice has been a significant factor underpinning this shift – although it has to be recognized that we still have a long way to go when it comes to integrating the worlds of knowledge dissemination (for example, universities) and knowledge use (for example, professional practice).

The knowledgeable doer

The 'knowledgeable doer' is a term widely used in nurse education. It refers to a practitioner who is, to use our terminology, able to integrate theory and practice. Although it has its roots in nursing, our view is that it is a concept that can apply across the helping professions and not just within health care settings. It is a helpful term in so far as it captures the idea that knowing and doing need to be connected. It can be linked to the philosophical term 'praxis', which is used to mean a fusion of theory and practice. It involves recognizing that theory and practice are two sides of the same coin – they do not exist in a pure form, independent of each other. Theorizing is an activity in itself and thus a form of practice in its own right, while practice is inevitably based on a theoretical knowledge base (a set of concepts that help us make sense of our experience), even though we may not always be aware of this (that is, we often take our theory base for granted). Griseri offers helpful comment in this regard:

> By 'praxis' I mean a personal theory-in-action that someone uses to get on with their life. Long before anyone learns anything about the formal theory of dynamics, they may learn how best to throw a stone so that it will skim along the top of a still pond.
>
> (1998, p. 213)

This helps us to understand that 'theory' need not be formal theory. Rather, the term 'theory' is used to refer to those concepts that we build up into a framework that helps us make sense of our lives in general and our work in particular. This framework forms the basis of our understanding and thus of our knowledge base. That knowledge base comprises both formal and informal knowledge (that is, knowledge gained from formal educational sources as well as from our life experiences). However, an even more important distinction is between open and closed knowledge. It is to this that we now turn.

Drawing on knowledge

Reflective practice, as we noted earlier, involves thinking, but not just any sort of thinking. It refers to thinking that helps us make sense of our practice, what is required of us, how best to respond and so on. As such, it is thinking that draws on knowledge. In a sense, all thinking draws on some form of knowledge, but the key question that concerns us here is: what type of knowledge are we drawing upon – open or closed?

Open knowledge is the type of knowledge that we have an explicit awareness of. It refers to situations where we are drawing on an *explicit* knowledge base, where we know precisely what knowledge we are using and why we think it is appropriate. For example, in dealing with someone who has been traumatized, we may be drawing directly on theory and research relating to the effects of trauma on individuals. Such knowledge is open to challenge and scrutiny, so that any flaws in it may become apparent, thus allowing the knowledge base to be improved and developed over time. Similarly, if we are openly aware of the knowledge we are using, we can increase that knowledge over time – we can continue to learn.

Closed knowledge, by contrast, is the type of knowledge we draw on implicitly, without any direct awareness of it. It arises in situations where we have acquired knowledge, but we are not sure what we have acquired or how we acquired it. For example, in dealing with someone who is agitated, we may calm them down very well, but without knowing how we did it or where we gained the knowledge of how to do so. Such knowledge is not explicit, and is therefore not open to the same level of scrutiny or challenge as explicit knowledge. And, if we are not aware of what knowledge we are using, how can we build that knowledge up? How can we continue to learn?

We can see, then, that open knowledge has distinct advantages over closed knowledge, although the latter is not entirely without its uses. The differences between the two can be summarized as follows.

Open knowledge is:

- Informed
- Sensitive
- Creative
- Rewarding
- Challenging of stereotypes and discriminatory assumptions
- A sound basis for working in partnership
- Empowering (of ourselves and others)
- Ethical; and
- Increases the chances of being effective.

Closed knowledge is:

- Uninformed
- Potentially insensitive
- Stifling
- Unrewarding
- Potentially reliant on stereotypes and discriminatory assumptions
- A dubious basis for working in partnership
- Potentially disempowering (of ourselves and others)
- Potentially unethical; and it
- Decreases the chances of being effective

Open knowledge is a basis for reflective, mindful practice, while closed knowledge runs the risk of being the basis for dogmatic and mindless practices. The value of focusing on developing open knowledge is therefore quite clear, as these comments from Karvinen-Niinikoski make clear:

> Open expertise recognizes uncertainty and, instead of claiming to be the only one to possess proper knowledge and professional skills, it will be ready to question communication and even polemics as well as a willingness to negotiate and reconstruct expertise according to the different contexts of action.
>
> (2004, p. 25)

In a similar vein, Gardner, Fook and White discuss 'open-mindedness' which fits well with our use of the term 'open knowledge' or Karvinen-Niinikoski's 'open expertise':

> Open-mindedness [is] an attitude of mind which actively welcomes suggestions and relevant information from all sides . . . The worst thing about stubbornness of mind, about prejudices, is that they arrest development; they shut off the mind from new stimuli. Open-mindedness means retention of the childlike attitude . . . Open-mindedness is not the same as empty-mindedness. To hang out a sign saying 'Come right in; there is no one at home' . . . But there is a kind of passivity, willingness to let experiences accumulate and sink in and ripen (Dewey 1916: 174–5).
>
> (2006, p. 228)

What we are advocating, then, is openness in three senses:

- *Open knowledge*: the explicit use of knowledge that is open to challenge and scrutiny and that will grow and develop over time as opposed to closed knowledge that is potentially dogmatic and a barrier to learning.
- *Open-mindedness*: in the sense used by Gardner, Fook and White of not having fixed or preconceived ideas – allowing scope for creativity; and
- *Openness to learning*: being willing to learn from not only our mistakes, but also from what we do well.

Voice of experience 1.2

I find it very difficult working with Steve. He is a very experienced practitioner and he clearly has a lot to offer, but I worry sometimes about how closed he is to new ideas or to learning. He seems to have such a macho attitude that seems to say 'I've seen it all, done it all and there's nothing anyone can teach me.' I think it's only a matter of time before he gets himself into serious difficulties one way or another.

Jen, a social worker in a multidisciplinary drugs and alcohol team

Using knowledge critically

Using knowledge is clearly, then, an important part of reflective practice. However, as some of our earlier comments indicate, it needs to be a *critical* use of knowledge – that is, one that:

(i)   does not accept the situation at face value and looks beneath the surface to see what assumptions and forms of reasoning are influencing the circumstances (critical *depth*); and

(ii) locates what is happening in its wider social context – that is, sees what processes are occurring at a micro level as part of a more holistic social and political picture at the macro level (critical *breadth*).

The critical use of knowledge therefore involves elements of both depth and breadth.

Moon refers to Proctor's (1993) emphasis on 'criticality' in reflective practice:

> On this view, reflective practice is the process of looking back in a critical way at what has occurred and using the results of this process, together with professional knowledge (with technical and ethical aspects), to tackle new situations.
>
> (1999, p. 59)

This helps us to understand that a critical perspective is one that can help us to develop a fuller understanding of the situations we face so that we are better equipped to deal with them. A critical perspective is a key part of what has come to be known as 'critical reflection', an important topic that is worthy of closer attention.

CRITICALLY REFLECTIVE PRACTICE

Some writers (for example, Fook and Askeland, 2006) draw a distinction between reflective practice and critical reflection. However, while respecting the important contribution of such writers, we prefer not to draw such a distinction, as, in our view, an approach to reflective practice that does not adopt a critical perspective would produce poor-quality practice and, in some respects, dangerous practice – for example, by unwittingly reinforcing patterns of discrimination. We therefore use the term *critically reflective practice* to emphasize that a critical 'edge' to both reflection and practice is an essential prerequisite. We also feel it is important to use the term 'practice' (that is, critically reflective *practice*, as opposed to simply critical reflection) to emphasize that reflective activities need to be directly part and parcel of the practice world and not an activity limited to educational programmes one or more steps removed from the day-to-day activities of practice.

What do we mean by 'critical'?

By critical we do not mean being unappreciative ('Lin was critical of Carol's efforts'), nor do we mean it in the sense of referring to a crisis point (the 'critical moment'). Rather, we mean it in the sense of an approach that is characterized by questioning and not taking things for granted – especially social arrangements that are based on inequality and disadvantage. As we noted above, it has both breadth and depth.

In relation to the depth aspect, Taylor provides helpful comment in stating that:

> According to Bandman and Bandman (1995: 7) critical thinking is 'the rational examination of ideas, inferences, statements, beliefs, and actions'. They clarify their definition by stating that critical thinking includes scientific reasoning, the use of the nursing process, decision-making and reasoning about issues. Adding further specifications to the definition, they make it clear that critical thinking is reasoning in which we analyse the use of language, formulate problems, clarify and explicate assumptions, weigh evidence, evaluate conclusions, discriminate between good and bad arguments, and seek to justify those facts that result in credible beliefs and actions.
>
> (2006, p. 105)

Members of other professions can substitute 'helping process' (Thompson, 2002) for 'nursing process' without losing the value of the points being made.

However, what Taylor is referring to here is only one part of criticality in the sense in which we are using it. While it covers the 'depth' element of a critical perspective (looking beneath the surface to see what assumptions and reasoning are being relied upon), we also need to consider the 'breadth' dimension – the wider sociopolitical aspects of the situation. Dolan, Canavan and Pinkerton give us a good indication of what this needs to entail:

> Gambrill, citing Brookfield, argues that reflection becomes critical when it has the purpose of unmasking how power underpins, frames and distorts processes and interaction. She also argues that critical thinking questions assumptions and practices that seem to make our lives easier but actually work against our long-term best interest.
>
> (2006. pp. 19–20)

This important passage highlights the breadth aspect by introducing the key concept of power but, in addition, refers to the depth aspect by highlighting that we also need to look at underlying assumptions.

Beyond atomism

The point was made earlier that Schön's work is predominantly individualistic in its focus – that is, it pays relatively little attention to the wider social context of professional practice. Moon refers to the work of Morrison (1996) which is:

> critical of the lack of concern for the social, political and ethical awareness and the emancipation that can emanate from reflective processes as described by Schön. Smyth (1989) supports this view. He describes the vision of professionals as a concern with the 'micro aspects' of a situation, as opposed to 'macro concerns' of political and ethical issues or the wider generalizations that might be made from events in professional practice.
>
> (1999, p. 50)

Atomism refers to the philosophical notion of regarding society as simply a collection of individuals, with little or no acknowledgement of the role of wider social processes and factors. For example, an atomistic understanding of crime would see it as purely a matter of individual (im)morality and would take no account of poverty, cultural and peer pressures, economic pressures, the significance of drug or alcohol problems or other such macro-level issues.

A critical approach to reflective practice is one that goes beyond such atomism and takes account of the wider social picture – in relation to, for example, racism, sexism, ageism and other such forms of discrimination. A critically reflective practitioner is therefore someone who is not only self-aware, but also socially and politically aware – able to 'tune in' to the bigger social picture that plays such an important part in shaping people's lives, the problems they experience and the potential solutions to those problems.

Transformative potential

In terms of critically reflective practice, an important thinker is Mezirow (1983) who writes of 'perspective transformation'. By this he means the way in which processes of reflection, when genuinely critical, can result in different understandings of a person's situation. This is parallel with the basis of narrative therapy in which people who have been disempowered by their circumstances (experiences of abuse, for example) can be helped to develop a more positive understanding and outlook by being supported in 'co-constructing a new narrative' – that is, being helped to create new meanings or understandings that are more empowering (for example, by transforming a negative 'victim' narrative into a more positive 'survivor' narrative).

Such a transformative perspective is also often referred to as an emancipatory approach – that is, one that helps to free people up from restrictive aspects of their social circumstances (discrimination, stigma, poverty and so on). Moon again offers helpful comment:

> Emancipatory interests rely on the development of knowledge via critical or evaluative modes of thought and enquiry so as to under- stand the self, the human condition and self in the human context. The acquisition of such knowledge is aimed at producing a transfor- mation in the self, or in the personal, social or world situation or any combination of these.
>
> (1999, p. 14)

Critically reflective practice can play a crucial part in trying to make sure that professional practice is geared towards positive, emancipatory outcomes, rather than reinforcing existing patterns of inequality and disadvantage.

Practice focus 1.3

Even though he was black himself, Marcus had given very little thought to racism in relation to mental health when he began his psychiatric nurse training. However, when it came to the point where he was required to spend some time on the wards as part of his training programme, he was amazed to find out that such a high propor- tion of the patients were from a minority ethnic background. He was also taken aback when, in having discussions with some of the black patients, he could see the signifi- cance of racism in terms of how their problems had developed and how they had subsequently been treated by both professionals and the general public. However, what surprised him most was that, when he read the files relating to the patients he had been talking to, he could see no mention of racism at all. Such matters did not appear to have been part of the assessments carried out by the psychiatrists, the nurses, the psychologists or the social workers. As a result of this he started to read up on racism and mental health. He started to appreciate that, while he had seen no specific evidence of personal racism on the part of any of the professionals, the almost total failure to recognize the significance of racism in black people's lives and their experience of mental distress was in itself a very worrying feature of the mental health system.

CONCLUSION

This chapter has set the scene for the following chapters by clarifying what we mean by reflective practice, and in particular, *critically* reflective practice. It has explored various aspects of the topic, many of which will be revisited and expanded upon in the pages that follow. It has also, we hope, given a clear picture of the complexities of reflective practice and the dangers of adopting a superficial or simplistic approach to the issues involved.

So, to return to the question that forms the title of the chapter (*What is reflective practice?*), we would find it difficult to improve on the helpful summary of some of the main elements involved provided by Brechin, Brown and Eby:

> Reflection is the ability to think and consider 'experiences, percept[ion]s, ideas [values and beliefs], etc. with a view to the discovery of new relations or the drawing of conclusions for the guidance of future action' (Quinn, 1998, p. 122). In other words, reflection enables individuals to make sense of their lived experiences through examining such experiences in context.
>
> Reflection, although a cornerstone of reflective practice, is not the only skill needed. Reflective practice is more than just a thoughtful practice. It is the process of turning thoughtful practice into a potential learning situation 'which may help to modify and change approaches to practice' (Schober, 1993, p. 324). Reflective practice entails the synthesis of self-awareness, reflection and critical thinking.
>
> (2000a, p. 52)

Having clarified our basic approach to reflective practice, we can now move on to explore three key dimensions of our topic: the cognitive, affective and value dimensions. These form the subject matter of Chapter 2 and so it is to these that we now turn.

Chapter 2

Dimensions of Reflection

INTRODUCTION

As we noted in Chapter 1, the traditional approach to reflective practice is one that has a strong rational emphasis, with little or no attention paid to the emotional issues involved. This can be seen as a significant omission as professional practice clearly has a number of emotional issues to address. We also noted that the traditional approach has relatively little to say about the wider social and political sphere. This chapter therefore seeks to go some way towards rectifying these imbalances. Here we present reflective practice as a three-dimensional entity, the three dimensions being:

- *Cognitive:* understanding the importance of thinking in general and analysis and creativity in particular.
- *Affective:* appreciating how significant emotional concerns are in shaping practice and how dangerous it can be to fail to take account of them.
- *Values:* becoming aware of the moral-political factors that are ever-present in our work and which should not be neglected.

We shall address each of these in turn below.

Clutterbuck makes an interesting point when he explains that:

> Data becomes useful when it is organised into information. Information becomes useful when it can be reconstructed into knowledge, which implies some degree of understanding of how information can be applied. When knowledge can be extrapolated beyond one set of circumstances, with understanding of broad principles, and linked to other relevant knowledge, it becomes wisdom.
>
> (1998, p. 90)

Gilbert (2004) makes a similar point about wisdom in stating that, while knowledge involves knowing that a tomato is a fruit, it is wisdom that tells us not to put tomatoes into a fruit salad. In other words, wisdom involves linking pieces of knowledge together in a way that is meaningful and relevant to our practice concerns. The reflective practitioner, then, should be seen as not simply a knowledgeable, thinking practitioner, but rather as a *wise* practitioner. Part of that wisdom, we would argue, is being able to handle all three dimensions of practice: cognitive, affective and moral-political.

THE COGNITIVE DIMENSION: THE POWER OF THOUGHT

Mindfulness: the thinking practitioner

'Mindfulness' is a term commonly used in eastern thought to refer to a heightened level of thinking – going above everyday thought processes. It involves training the spotlight of our consciousness on what we see as the important issues, focusing clearly on the key elements of the situation. Moon shows that this is not a new idea:

> Dewey (1933) allies reflection with thinking and uses a number of terms for it. He describes it as 'the kind of thinking that consists in turning a subject over in the mind and giving it serious thought'. Reflection is a chain of linked ideas that aims at a conclusion and is more than a stream of consciousness. The anticipated end to be reached determines the process of operations that lead to it. In this respect, the anticipated outcome could be said to coincide with the purpose of reflection.
>
> (1999, p. 12)

This is the type of thinking that we associate with reflective practice – deliberative thinking and more than just everyday thoughts. It is sometimes referred to as 'surfacing', which involves bringing things to the surface – in other words, making the implicit explicit. As such, it is an important part of reflective practice.

We can also link it to philosophical thinking (philosophy being the love or pursuit of wisdom) for, as Christenson points out: 'Philosophy is disciplined critical reflection (about fundamental ideas) that spring from wonder' (2001, p. vii). 'Wonder', as a concept, then brings us back to mindfulness and indeed to wisdom. Christenson goes on to say:

> Wonder usually occurs not the first time we experience something but the first time we really see what we have looked at a thousand times but have never stopped to notice before. Wonder occurs experientially but can also occur conceptually, when we understand (or see that we do not understand) something in a new way. Wonder is the experience of the familiar as suddenly unfamiliar, the encounter with the usual in a way that suddenly makes it shockingly new and fresh.
>
> (2001, pp. 5–6)

Mindfulness can therefore be seen as the use of wonder to lead us to wisdom. It involves avoiding falling into the trap of thinking in tramlines, simply following routinized patterns of thought and thus standardized forms of practice. Relying on habit, routine and uncritical acceptance of the status quo is not a sound basis for reflective practice – quite the opposite. Reflective practice is, in part, intended as an antidote to these problems.

This question of habit, routine and uncritical acceptance is doubly important. This is because:

(i)   It can prevent mindful thinking from developing; if we are engaged in 'tramline thinking'. It is very easy for our critical faculties to be turned off and the BOB problem to emerge. What we mean by the BOB problem is that, if we are not careful, our practice 'Bypasses Our Brain' – we go about our business in ways that do not involve thinking about the issues we face and working out how best to deal with them. We can easily fall into the trap of standardized, knee-jerk responses to situations that can get us, our organizations and the people we are seeking to help into serious difficulties. The BOB problem is therefore the equivalent of going onto automatic pilot, and that is clearly a dangerous step to take in the helping professions. It shows a distinct lack of respect for the people we serve, and therefore raises some significant values issues to which we shall return below. Tramline thinking and the BOB problem often arise when people are under high levels of pressure but, as we noted in Chapter 1, the busier we are, the more reflective we need to be.

(ii) It can act as a barrier to developing creative solutions and more effective ways of working. We shall examine below the importance of creativity as a feature of reflective practice, but for now we should note that habit and routine, if relied upon too much, can be highly counterproductive.

Practice focus 2.1

Marion was a nurse employed in a nursing home for older people. She found the work quite demanding, with quite a lot to do, but it was also rewarding and, for the most part, enjoyable work that she was called upon to do. However, one day, she found that, of the complement of five nurses due to be on duty, two were off sick and, due to a breakdown in communication, no arrangements had been made for relief cover. So, in effect, until the afternoon shift came on duty, there were three staff doing the work of five. Marion realized that, in the circumstances, she would need to roll her sleeves up and make the best of a bad situation. She was not pleased about what had happened, but she did not see it as an insurmountable problem.

However, at one point in the morning she realized that she had completed giving out the medications to the residents she was responsible for, but she was so flustered by all the work she had to do that she had carried out this task without concentrating on it. Looking back, she recognized that she must have done it on 'automatic pilot', and it dawned on her just how dangerous this was, as giving somebody the wrong medication, or the wrong dose of the right medication, could prove disastrous. This time nothing untoward came of this lapse in her concentration, but she felt very anxious and concerned about what could have happened as a result of her falling into the trap of relying on unthinking routines.

Analytical thinking

In its literal sense, analysis means breaking things down into their component parts. For example, a chemical analysis would identify what chemical elements are present in a particular substance and in what proportions. However, the term is often used in a broader sense than this to mean examining a situation to make sense of it. It is in this sense that it is an important component of reflective practice. It involves drawing out recurring themes and issues and recognizing patterns that help us form a meaningful picture of the situation. Analytical thinking can be facilitated by asking ourselves some important questions, not least the following:

■ What type of situation am I dealing with here?

■ What are the key issues I need to be aware of (in particular, are there any dangers)?

■ What is happening? What processes are shaping what is happening?

■ What do other people expect of me here? Is this consistent with my professional role and the specific duties of my job? If not, what negotiation needs to take place to remedy the situation?

■ Do I have the information I need to act? If not, what do I need to find out and how?

■ Who else needs to be involved? Who do I need to communicate with?

■ What options are available in terms of dealing with this situation? How do I evaluate those options?

■ Are there any values issues here I need to consider (for example, showing respect, maintaining confidentiality, valuing diversity)?

These questions are not intended as a prescriptive framework for practitioners to follow (that would not be consistent with the spirit of reflective practice), but rather as an indication of the types of question that can be helpful in enabling us to make sense of the situations we are dealing with and framing a well-informed, carefully considered response. What we want to encourage is an analytical approach to practice, in the sense that practitioners make the most of their mental capacities in dealing with the challenges involved in our work in the helping professions.

In this regard, Dewey's (1933) comments are helpful. He describes reflective thinking as:

> Active, persistent and careful consideration of any belief or supposed form of knowledge in the light of the grounds that support it and further conclusions to which it leads . . . it includes a conscious and voluntary effort to establish belief upon a firm basis of evidence and rationality.
>
> (cited in Moon, 1999, p. 12)

Of course, it would not be realistic to adopt an analytical approach to everything we do. What is necessary, then, is the ability to distinguish between those circumstances that can safely be dealt with in a routine way and those that need a more focused, analytical approach. Being able to distinguish between these two types of situations is in itself an analytical skill and one worth developing over time (it is also something that supervisors, mentors or coaches can play a useful role in helping to develop – see the discussion of these issues in Chapter 3).

Clearly we are dealing with some complex issues here. Doyle helps to cast some light on the situation when she argues that:

Thinking theoretically without any form of reflection becomes rigidity of thought, which leads ultimately to unthinking intervention, whereas reflection without any sort of theoretical basis is woolly thinking, which also leads ultimately to unthinking intervention. Unthinking intervention becomes habitual intervention, which in turn leads to ineffective practice.

(2006, p. 15)

As we saw in Chapter 1, theoretical understanding is important. However, as Doyle indicates, such understanding is no substitute for reflective analysis. What is needed, if we are to avoid unthinking, habitual and ineffective practice, is a foundation of theoretical knowledge that is then subjected to critical analysis (that is, the theoretical knowledge base provides the cloth, reflective analysis provides the tailoring).

Our powers of analysis can be helped by making use of what is referred to as 'dialectical' thinking. 'The dialectic' refers to the process of interacting forces producing a new outcome. For example, pressures towards change can encounter pressures to maintain the status quo, resulting in an outcome that is a blend of the old and the new – or to put it in technical terms: a thesis encounters an antithesis and the result is a synthesis. Going back to the point made earlier that analysis literally means breaking things down into their component parts, dialectical thinking involves linking them together to get a more holistic picture. Our thinking therefore needs to be analytical in the broader sense of enabling us to make sense of the overall picture, rather than in the narrower sense of simply breaking things down into their component parts. In other words, there needs to be a dialectical element to our thinking, one that incorporates notions of change, conflict and interaction (that is, we are dealing with moving pictures and not snapshots). Such a dialectical approach is also useful in helping us build up the type of holistic picture that is needed for *critically* reflective practice.

The helping professions are a part of a complex, changing world, based on a mixture of consensus and conflict. We therefore have to make sure that our understanding is sufficiently sophisticated and dynamic to do it justice.

Creative thinking

Earlier we noted the significance of wonder, in the sense of being able to look at familiar situations in a new light. This is an important way of avoiding getting bogged down in routine, standardized ways of working that have limited effectiveness, that are demotivating (and thus a potential contributor to stress) and that act as barriers to learning and development. Wonder is a foundation for creative thinking, and creative thinking will stimulate and support wonder.

Griseri discusses similar issues:

> Ellen Langer talks of the negative effects of taking things for granted, which she calls 'mindlessness'. In contrast, she points out how creativity and greater understanding can often be stimulated by focusing on what one has always accepted and regarding it as no longer certain.
>
> (1998, p. 17)

Without creativity, we face a fate of getting stuck in a rut of routine practices that are likely to have limited effectiveness and also run the risk of communicating to the people we are trying to help an unintended (but none the less very powerful) message that they are not important, that they do not merit more than a standardized, unimaginative response. This is clearly not a sound foundation for working in the helping professions. As the saying goes: 'If you always do what you've always done, you'll always get what you always got.' In other words, an approach lacking in creativity will close off avenues for helping and make us largely ineffectual in making a real positive difference to people's lives.

In a similar vein, Hamer makes the important point that: 'If our own creativity is stifled, then it becomes difficult to foster the creativity in others that encourages them to pursue the kinds of lives they hope to have' (2006, p. ix). This means that, without creativity, any efforts geared towards empowerment will be significantly hampered. There is therefore an increased risk of creating dependency which, in turn, can lead to increased pressures on services and the professionals involved in providing and commissioning them, thus making everybody's life more difficult. This can then lead to a vicious circle in which people claim that, because of these pressures, they do not have time to be reflective; they must just 'get on with it'.

One common barrier to creativity is the stereotype that being creative means being artistic. If we look back over history, we can see that some of the most creative people in history have been scientists rather than artists, and so a lack of artistic skills should not be seen as an obstacle to creativity. Creativity involves being able to look at situations from different angles, not allowing the familiar and habitual to blind us to other opportunities or avenues for helping. To a large extent, creative thinking is an extension of analytical thinking.

We can also link creative thinking to critical thinking for, as Christenson comments:

> Any society that values creativity also needs to enable criticism. If we cannot question the way we are doing things and thinking about things at present, it will not occur to us that they could be thought of or done differently.
>
> (2001, p. 37)

We can now see a pattern here. Reflection involves thinking, and such thinking needs to be analytical, creative and critical – three types of thinking that support and reinforce each other.

THE AFFECTIVE DIMENSION: REFLECTING ON FEELINGS

Thinking is clearly important, but so too is feeling. We would be missing a significant dimension of our work if we were to neglect how crucial a role emotions play in shaping the problems people face and their responses to them.

Benner, Hooper-Kyriakidis and Stannard (1999) illustrate how emotion is something we need to consider in addition to the rational aspects, and not instead of:

> Traditionally, emotion has been seen as opposed to cognition and rationality. But increasingly, it is recognized that emotions play a key role in perception and even act as a moral compass in learning and practice (Dreyfus, Dreyfus and Benner, 1996).
>
> (1999, p. 15)

Reflective practice therefore needs to incorporate an element of reflecting on the emotional foundations and implications of our work. To facilitate this we shall comment on five aspects of the emotional dimension, we begin by exploring the important, but often misunderstood distinction between empathy and sympathy.

Sympathy vs. empathy

Sympathy involves sharing someone's feelings. That is, if they are sad, we become sad. If they are disappointed, we become disappointed. Empathy, by contrast, is where we recognize someone's feelings but we do not necessarily share them. For example, we may see that someone is grieving but without necessarily grieving ourselves. While sympathy is an understandable response to many of the situations we encounter in the helping professions, empathy is what we should be aiming for. This is because sympathy can leave us ill-equipped for the range and intensity of emotions we are likely to encounter. We would quickly become worn down and therefore of very little use to anyone if we experienced the feelings we encounter in our work.

Empathy is a more realistic option. It involves being emotionally aware – sensitive to what people are going through – but without allowing the emotions to affect us. Pure empathy is, of course, not possible, as some situations will inevitably evoke an emotional response in us – we would not be human if this did not occur. However, what we should aim for is getting as close to empathy as we can.

Voice of experience 2.1

When I first became involved in counselling I found it very difficult indeed. I felt for every client and started to take on board the pain and confusion they were expressing to me. Steadily I could feel myself becoming overloaded with all the emotion. When I raised the issue with my supervisor she was very helpful and reminded me of the importance of empathy not sympathy. She made me realize that I had allowed myself to slip into a sympathetic way of working rather than an empathetic way. It was a tough job making the transition, but I recognized that I had to – I couldn't go on the way I was; it would have done me a lot of harm and would also have meant that I was less help to my clients.

Rhian, a counsellor at a GP surgery

In order to be able to rely on empathy rather than sympathy we need to be 'tuned in' to other people's emotions, able to recognize indicators of a person's emotional state (tone of voice and body language, for example). However, we also need to be 'tuned in' to our own emotional responses – aware of how the emotional aspects of a situation are affecting us. This is a form of self-awareness and, as such, an important part of reflective practice.

Emotional intelligence

Being tuned in to other people's feelings as well as our own is precisely what emotional intelligence is all about. The term 'emotional intelligence' has become quite a popular one in recent years, widely used in literature relating to management and business. Unfortunately, it is often used in a simplistic sense, showing a relatively superficial understanding of the complexities of emotional life. Despite this, however, the basic concept remains fundamentally a useful one.

Being 'emotionally intelligent' involves being able to 'read' other people's emotions – to be able to recognize the subtle cues in their language and behaviour that give us important messages about their emotional state. This then gives us a platform for deciding how best to respond. If we are clued in to the ways in which emotions are affecting people, we are in a stronger position to help them, as we will have a more insightful understanding of their circumstances. For example, if we know that someone is feeling disorientated because of significant changes taking place in their life, we will be able to work out that they are likely to find it helpful if we are able to provide some sort of anchor or stability for them.

The other side of the emotional intelligence coin is being 'in touch' with our own feelings – that is, being able to appreciate what we are feeling and why we are feeling that way. For example, we may feel negative towards somebody because we are envious of something they have, but we may not fully realize that these feelings of envy are influencing our behaviour and attitudes towards that individual. This is another aspect of self-awareness, being able to recognize what feelings are currently affecting us and how significant they may be.

Emotional intelligence is not something we can develop overnight. It is something which, if we do not have it already, can take a long time to develop. However, its value to us in the helping professions certainly repays the time and effort required to maximize our potential in this area. If we are not sufficiently attuned to the emotional aspects of our work, then we run the risk of:

- Being insensitive to the needs of the people we are trying to help and thus decreasing the likelihood of success and increasing the chances of doing harm.
- Missing significant factors that may need to be addressed before we can make progress.
- Failing in our duty of self-care – that is, putting ourselves in situations that may be emotionally harmful to us (in dealing with people who have been traumatized, for example – see Warren, 2006).
- Failing to support colleagues by not recognizing any emotional issues that may be causing them difficulty.

So, regardless of the rather simplistic claims of some adherents of emotional intelligence, it is a concept that we need to take seriously.

Anxiety and uncertainty

Jobs that involve working with people inevitably involve a degree of uncertainty. This is because, while the social sciences have taught us about various common patterns of behaviour that enable us to make reasonable predictions about how people are likely to act and interact in certain circumstances, the degree of uncertainty and unpredictability remains high. Working with people therefore involves working with uncertainty. As Moon puts it:

> the reflective practitioner with a self-image as a facilitator, for whom there is important recognition of the uncertainty of the professional situation, the knowledge base of the profession and, thereby, the problems that need to be resolved in practice, the reflective practitioner will cope with this uncertainty by putting the relationship with the client at the centre of practice with an attempt reflectively to develop negotiated and shared meanings and under-standings as a joint process.
>
> (1999, pp. 62–3)

This is wise advice that we would support. It links well with the notion of partnership, an important concept we shall discuss in more detail below.

Linked to uncertainty is the issue of anxiety. A certain degree of anxiety is only to be expected and is not necessarily a problem – indeed, it can be helpful (for example, by keeping us alert and focused, keeping complacency at bay). However, too much anxiety can be debilitating, creating problems not only for ourselves, but also for our colleagues and for those we are seeking to help. It is therefore important that we manage to keep our anxiety within manageable limits. We can do this by:

■ Recognizing that a degree of anxiety is normal and acceptable – if we feel bad about experiencing anxiety, we can develop a vicious circle in which our anxiety grows and grows, sapping our confidence.
■ Trying to clarify what precisely we are afraid of – having this clarity can help us to manage our anxieties (see Thompson, 2006b).
■ Identify the sources of support you can draw upon. The support of others can make a huge difference when it comes to keeping anxiety in check.

Dealing with our own anxiety is, of course, only half the battle. We also need to give careful consideration to the skills involved in supporting others through their anxiety. Developing our emotional intelligence, as discussed above, can be a good first step in that direction.

Grief

A common misunderstanding of grief is that it is primarily if not exclusively a reaction to bereavement – that is, a response to the death of someone close to us. The reality is that grief arises in response to any significant loss, regardless of whether death is involved: divorce or other relationship breakdown; redundancy or retirement; a child leaving home; an elderly person moving into a care home; becoming disabled; and so on. This means that grief is a much more common emotion than many people realize. It is often at the root of many of the problems we frequently encounter in the helping professions: depression; anger and aggression; self-harm; interpersonal conflicts; and so on.

One of the implications of this is that we need to be careful to make sure that we do not fall into the trap of failing to recognize grief and its effects. Even someone who is grieving may not realize that this is what is happening to them – they may not be able to make the connection between their experience of one or more losses and the way they are feeling. For example, someone who is grieving can have intense feelings of guilt, even though they have nothing to feel guilty about. Even where we recognize that such strong feelings of guilt are a normal response to a major loss, they can be very difficult to deal with. However, where the person concerned does not make this connection and recognize the feelings of guilt as part of a grief reaction, the feelings will be even more difficult to deal with – possibly leading to considerable distress.

And, of course, this does not only apply to the people we seek to help; we are not immune to such difficulties ourselves. If we are not sufficiently aware of the significance of grief as a reaction to any major loss, we may struggle to cope with our duties due to the emotional impact of our circumstances. Being able to understand what is happening to us when we go through an emotionally turbulent time can be very helpful, and so having a greater sensitivity to the prevalence and impact of grief on people's lives is a distinct advantage.

It is understandable that, given the emotional sensitivity and intensity involved in situations of loss and grief, some people will feel uncomfortable in dealing with the issues that arise and will perhaps seek to avoid engaging with them. However, while we can appreciate the temptation to do this, we can also see how dangerous such an approach can be, as it means that vitally important issues may not be addressed, significant avenues for helping may not be pursued and we may be giving a message that we do not care – just at

LIBRARY, UNIVERSITY OF CHESTER

a time when those affected perhaps need help and support more than ever. The self-awareness we earlier identified as an important part of reflective practice therefore needs to incorporate awareness of our own reactions to other people's grief – to make sure that we do not allow our own discomfort to predominate at the expense of the person or persons who need help.

Practice focus 2.2

Omar was surprised to encounter such an aggressive reaction when he went to visit the Leighton family. He had helped them make arrangements for Mrs Leighton's mother to be admitted to a residential home, as she could no longer cope in the community, even with extensive family and social services support. Throughout the process they had been polite and welcoming and had thanked him for his help and understanding. However, when he went to see them to sort out some of the final administrative details after the admission had taken place, their attitude had changed. They seemed very on edge and very different from how they had been before. Before he had had time to fill in the necessary details on the forms, they had become quite aggressive towards him, as if they were blaming him for the situation. He was very puzzled by this and started racking his brains to try and work out what he had done to upset or antagonize them. He felt very uncomfortable with this and it clearly knocked his confidence. He was so concerned that he raised the issue with his line manager in a supervision session. Fortunately, his line manager was someone who was quite tuned in to grief issues and was able to recognize the aggressive attitude as a feature of Mr and Mrs Leighton's grief reaction as a result of the major change in their life. Once Omar understood this he felt so much better, knowing that it wasn't his fault and now feeling much more confident about how to help them. He realized that this had been a valuable lesson for him to learn, but wished he had been able to learn it in a less painful way.

Gender, culture and emotion

Traditionally, emotion has been conceptualized as primarily a biological matter. It tends to be seen as a physiological reaction to life events. However, there is now a growing literature on the social aspects of emotion. For example, Williams argues that a useful starting point is:

> to see emotions as complex, multifaceted human compounds which arise, sociologically speaking, in a variety of sociorelational contexts, including fundamental processes of management, differentiation and change linking larger social structures with the emotional

> experiences and expressions of embodied individuals (Gordon
> 1990). This in turn suggests the need . . . to work 'both ways' so to
> speak, from the social shaping of emotions by social structure to
> the emotional shaping of social structure itself (ibid.).
>
> (2001, p. 1)

To this we can add the interrelationship between emotions and culture, rather than just structure, thus creating an even more complex picture. What this complexity tells us is that it is a mistake to see emotion simply as a biological response. While emotion no doubt has a biological dimension, it also has psychological and sociological dimensions. We therefore have to be very aware that emotional responses will be influenced to a large extent by such key factors as culture and gender.

In reflecting on the emotional dimension of our work, it is therefore essential that we take account of differences in cultural expression and interpretation of emotion and different gender experiences of emotion. These are very complex issues, and space does not permit a detailed analysis of what is involved. You are therefore advised to consult the *Guide to Further Learning* at the end of the book, where you will find suggestions for further reading around these very complex, but very important issues.

Voice of experience 2.2

I knew that dealing with the emotional side of my work would be difficult, but, until I started my formal training I hadn't realized how complex emotions are. For example, I had assumed that men and women grieve in the same way, so I was amazed to find that there is research to show that there are often significant gender differences in how people deal with their losses. It came as quite a surprise to me to learn that – and that was before we went on to look at how emotions operate in subtly different ways in different cultures! I could see that I would have my work cut out in making sense of it all.

Aoife, a hospice worker

THE VALUES DIMENSION: REFLECTING ON VALUES

Moss makes the point that: 'Without an awareness of values, our practice can become dangerous' (2007, p. 3). This is something with which we would wholeheartedly concur. Values shape not only our thoughts and feelings, but also our actions. Therefore, if we are not aware of what values are influencing these three important dimensions of our practice, we are largely working in the dark – and that is something that is clearly not consistent with the philosophy of reflective practice.

Reflecting on values is therefore something we see as a crucial basis of high-quality professional practice. It involves asking ourselves such questions as:

■ What are the values associated with my profession (as identified in codes of practice and other such official documentation)?
■ What do these mean to me in practice?
■ What are my personal values?
■ What do these mean to me in practice?
■ Are there any conflicts between these two sets of values?
■ Are there any conflicts between these values and how I practise?
■ How can I safeguard my personal and professional values if they are under threat in some way?

This is not an exhaustive list, but it should be enough to show that there are some very important issues relating to values that we ignore at our peril.

In the remainder of this chapter we explore some of the key issues that arise when it comes to reflecting on the values dimension of our work. We recognize that different professional groups will have different conceptions of their respective value bases and different priorities and emphases. We shall therefore concentrate on three sets of values issues that we see as applicable across the board in the helping professions, regardless of specific discipline background. These are: partnership, empowerment and equality and diversity.

Partnership

This is a term that has become widely used in the helping professions in recent years. There has been much written and spoken about the need to work in partnership. Ideas like 'joined-up thinking for joined-up working' have become established. However, what has been confusing is that:

(i) There has been insufficient discussion of what we actually mean by 'partnership' or how we are to put it into practice – the term has crept into our vocabulary, often without people having the opportunity to explore together its precise meaning and its implications (for example, we have been involved in running training courses on partnership in which it has become apparent that there is far more confusion about partnership than there is clarity).

(ii) The term is often used in two separate but related senses. It can refer to (a) multidisciplinary collaboration (how do different professional groups work together effectively to produce the best outcomes for the people we serve?); and (b) the nature of the working relationship between professional practitioners and the person(s) receiving help (how can we make sure that professional practice is about doing things *with* people, not *to* or *for* them?).

In terms of the relationship between worker and client/patient/service user, Schön provides a helpful picture in distinguishing between two types of 'contract' – that is, agreement about the basis of the working relationship:

Traditional Contract

I put myself into the professional's hands and, in doing this, I gain a sense of security based on faith.

I have the comfort of being in good hands. I need only comply with his [sic] advice and all will be well.

I am pleased to be served by the best person available.

Reflective Contract

I join with the professional in making sense of my case, and in doing this I gain a sense of increased involvement and action.

I can exercise some control over the situation. I am not wholly dependent on him; he is dependent on information and action that only I can undertake.

I am pleased to be able to test my judgements about his competence. I enjoy the excitement of discovery about his knowledge, about the phenomena of his practice, and about myself.

(Schön, 1983, p. 302)

This is a very telling passage as it shows a distinct move away from traditional 'we know best' models of professionalism, towards more reflective, partnership-based models in which we work together to find solutions, enable progress and so on. This is consistent with the emphasis on user involvement and citizen participation in health, welfare and related services in particular and with empowerment in general (see below). Partnership, in the sense of more egalitarian, inclusive and participatory approaches to working relationships with our clientele, is therefore entirely consistent with reflective practice.

Partnership and reflective practice are also compatible bedfellows at the broader level of partnership – that is, in relation to multidisciplinary collaboration. Being clear about what we are doing, why we are doing it, how we might work together, what might stand in the way of our working together and related matters are all bread and butter issues for multidisciplinary partnership, but they are also important features of reflective practice. There is, therefore, a strong linkage between partnership and multidisciplinary partnership.

Empowerment

Empowerment is another term that is now widely used, but not necessarily with a degree of understanding that matches the extent of its popularity as a concept. Our view of empowerment is that the helping professions are primarily about helping people to help themselves. That is, it is not about making people dependent – dependency should be a last resort and, even where it exists at all, it should be kept to a minimum, with the people concerned having as much control over their circumstances as possible. Empowerment, then, is about supporting people in having as much control over their lives and circumstances as they can. This involves identifying barriers at different levels – for example:

- **Personal.** This will include low self-esteem or confidence; fears and anxieties about failure (perhaps based on earlier negative experiences); and conflicting pressures.
- **Cultural.** Stereotypes that stigmatize and demean certain groups of people would be included among the factors that inhibit empowerment at a cultural level.

■ **Structural**. Social structures (based on race, class and gender) can have the effect of excluding certain groups and individuals from opportunities to control their own destiny.

Being reflective puts us in a stronger position to be able to help people overcome (or at least minimize) these and related obstacles. A non-reflective approach, by contrast may prove to be very disempowering. For example, if we are rushing around unreflectively 'getting on with the job', without considering the implications of our actions in terms of whether we are contributing to or undermining empowerment, then we may actually be doing more harm than good (contributing to low levels of confidence; unwittingly relying on stereotypes; and perhaps also reinforcing structural inequalities).

Empowerment, then, can be seen as part of our emphasis on *critically* reflective practice, in the sense that uncritical, mindless practice based on habit and routine will fail to address the significant personal, social and political obstacles to progress that stand in the way of people gaining greater control over their lives. Critically reflective practice can be very empowering, whereas uncritical, unreflective practice can be dangerously disempowering and thus potentially quite oppressive – something that is clearly not appropriate in the helping professions.

Moon also links critically reflective practice with empowerment:

> criticality has been widely associated with reflective practice and is taken to be the main purpose for reflection (Smyth, 1989), but it can mean different things – a critical view of the content of an action . . . or of the self or of the context of the professional or profession. Smyth (1989) provides an example of the third of these and provides a set of guiding questions as a basis for reflection to empower and politicize professionals in teaching.
>
> (1999, p. 59)

The term 'politicize' used here is an important one. It does not mean converting someone to a particular political viewpoint or party position. Rather, it means helping people to appreciate that professional practice and the problems such practice seeks to address do not occur in a political vacuum. To have an adequate understanding of our professional world, we need to be able to appreciate the political aspects of that world – this is a fundamental part of critically reflective practice.

In Chapter 1, we discussed the importance of reflective practice having transformative potential – that is, that it can in certain circumstances free people up from restrictive and self-limiting understandings of the situation they find themselves in (or indeed of their lives as a whole). The work of Mezirow is again relevant here:

> Mezirow talks of people being trapped in their meaning perspective and unable to develop as people. He sees some of the mission of adult education as being to emancipate people from a self-imposed restrictive view of the world to one that is open to new ideas and the changes in their lives that these may imply. The possibility of a change in a person's life view is encompassed in the notion of trans-formation.
>
> (Moon, 1999, p. 109)

This passage refers to the empowering potential of adult education. However, we would see it as being equally applicable across the helping professions (that is, including, but not limited to, adult education). Much of what we do in our work will put us in a position where we can have some degree of influence over a person's worldview. If their perspective is a self-disempowering, self-limiting one, then we will need to give careful consideration to what part we may be able to play (large or small) in influencing that worldview in a more positive, self-enhancing direction.

Equality and social justice

A key part of the idea of critically reflective practice is a commitment to seeing the 'big picture', including the wider social and political aspects of the situations we are dealing with, and indeed of our professional roles more broadly. This, then, will include such issues a social justice and equality. It would not make sense to adopt a holistic approach that does not recognize the significance of discrimination and oppression in so many people's lives.

What, then, can reflective practice contribute to efforts to promote equality and social justice?

One important contribution relates to the role of reflective practice in questioning the familiar and looking beneath the surface of what is so often taken for granted. This use of 'wonder', as we referred to it earlier, is a vital part of understanding such processes as discrimination and the oppression to which they lead. This is because discrimination is not simply a matter of the overt use of prejudicial behaviour towards others. As we have known for some time, the reality is much more complex than this. Discrimination is often 'institutionalized' – that is, it is built into our working lives (and indeed personal lives) at both cultural and structural levels (if you are not familiar with this more complex understanding of discrimination, see the *Guide to Further Learning* at the end of the book.) Reflective practice helps us to become attuned to the subtle processes that can lead to people being excluded, marginalized, stigmatized or otherwise disadvantaged – through, for example, the use of discriminatory forms of language.

An example of such a subtle process would be a situation in which assessments relating to, say, women offenders, make detailed reference to whether or not they have children and what significance this may have, while assessments relating to male offenders make little or no reference to such matters. What is so important about this is that a non-reflective approach to such issues not only reflects the discriminatory assumptions that are prevalent in society, but also reinforces them. We therefore have to make sure that we have a well-informed approach to these issues, otherwise there is a significant danger that our efforts to help may not only fail to tackle problems of discrimination and the injustices these create, but they may also make matters worse – for example, by increasing the level or impact of the discrimination.

Furthermore, it needs to be recognized that the discrimination many people encounter (for example, in relation to race/ethnicity, gender, age, sexuality, disability, language or class) will often be not only an additional problem alongside the primary problem that has necessitated professional intervention, it may also be a cause (or at least causal factor) in that problem. For example, an older person who is depressed may be experiencing such depression in large part because of ageism and its tendency to demean older people, to devalue their contribution to society and to produce low levels of expectations in terms of what joy, pleasure, pride and satisfaction older people can reasonably anticipate.

Equality and social justice are important goals to pursue in the helping professions (we can hardly claim to be helping and caring if, at best, we ignore significant sources of discrimination in so many people's lives and, at worst, actually make the discrimination worse). However, they are also very complex and subtle issues. Trying to tackle them without a proper understanding of what is involved and without a sensitivity to the nuances that can be so significant is likely to be doomed to failure. What is needed, then, is a well-informed approach that is attuned to the subtleties and complexities involved – in other words, a critically reflective approach.

Practice focus 2.3
Rob used to work with a man who was overtly racist and had little or no respect for women, for gay people or indeed for any minority. He had a very closed mind and narrow, prejudicial perspective on such matters. In his current job, by contrast, he witnessed no such overt prejudice or discrimination, but this did not mean that discrimination was not taking place. He was part of a multidisciplinary team working with disabled adults. He personally had a strong commitment to disability equality, as did many of his colleagues. However, some colleagues, those he would describe as 'old school', while not overtly discriminatory, would often make some quite discriminatory assumptions. On one occasion, he was quite shocked to find that one of his colleagues had expressed doubt about a romantic relationship a disabled man had begun to form with a non-disabled woman. It became clear from the ensuing conversation that this colleague was assuming that a disabled person should not have expectations of finding love and romance. Rob thought this was a very patronizing attitude and out of touch with reality. His colleague was shocked to be criticized by Rob in this way, but at least it did make him begin to consider whether he was being fair in making such assumptions about disabled people's sexuality and what they could expect in terms of forming and sustaining relationships.

CONCLUSION

This chapter has built on the foundations laid in Chapter 1. It has tried to take forward our understanding of critically reflective practice by examining three key dimensions: the cognitive aspects related to thinking and understanding; the affective aspects related to how feelings play an important role; and the values aspects related to the moral-political context of professional practice. We hope that we have given a clear picture of just how important each of these areas is, and how dangerous and problematic it would be if we were to neglect them.

What we also need to emphasize is the interrelationship of these three areas – they do not operate independently of each other. What we think will be influenced by what we feel and by our values. What we feel will be shaped in large part by what we think and, again, by our values. And, of course, our values and our attempts to live and work in accordance with them will owe much to our thoughts and feelings. In turn, all three dimensions – thoughts, feelings and values – will be major influences on our actions, our actual practice.

It should be clear, then, that a good understanding of all three dimensions is a necessary underpinning for high-quality critically reflective practice. It is to be hoped that this chapter has provided a sound foundation for developing that understanding.

Chapter 3

Contexts for Reflection

INTRODUCTION

Chapter 2 was divided into three main sections, each relating to an important dimension of reflection. Chapter 3 is also divided into three main sections, this time relating to three different *contexts* for reflection. The structure is based on Clutterbuck's comments when he argues that:

> An important factor here is the creation of reflective space – time to focus on thinking, understanding and learning instead of doing. Reflective space is important at three levels: personal (quiet thinking time on one's own); dyadic (one-to-one); and as a group or team.
>
> (1998, p. 15)

Our subject matter in this chapter is therefore concerned with these three sets of contextual issues:

- **Personal reflective space.** How can I maximize my potential for guiding my own reflection and promoting my own critically reflective practice?
- **Dyadic reflective space.** How can supervision, coaching or mentoring be put to best use in terms of promoting critically reflective practice?
- **Group learning space.** How can we maximize the positive outcomes in terms of promoting reflective practice by the use of group learning experiences (training courses, for example)?

We shall explore each of these important areas in turn.

PERSONAL REFLECTIVE SPACE

While there are important organizational implications for developing reflective practice that we feel managers and policymakers should take very seriously, there is also the individual professional responsibility that each of us has to make our practice as reflective as possible. Sometimes we will have the support of others (through supervision or group learning opportunities, for example), but much will depend on our ability to make reflection a reality within our own working practices as part of our basic duties and responsibilities. In this section, then, we explore what individual practitioners can do to develop critically reflective practice.

Clutterbuck's (1998) notion of personal reflective space refers to our capacity to take issues forward in terms of the critical analysis and understanding that underpin reflective practice. Here we shall look at five different aspects of how we can make it a reality.

Managing work pressures

Hamer makes the very important point that:

> Work is what we do with most of our waking lives. Work is central to our happiness and feelings of self-worth. We see ourselves reflected in our work, in the outcome and importance of what we do. When we think about our lives we often define ourselves in terms of how we make a living. We spend an enormous part of our life working, trying to make a living and trying to express our individuality.
>
> (2006, p. 4)

We would therefore be very foolish to ignore the significance of work in our lives. A key element of this is the ability to manage effectively the pressures we face within our particular work setting. If we struggle to keep our pressures under control, then we will also struggle to create personal space for reflection.

The irony here, as we noted in Chapter 1, is that, if we do not manage to be reflective, then we will have difficulty in managing our work pressures. This can then create a vicious circle, in so far as a non-reflective approach can mean that we miss important opportunities to take things forward, we make more mistakes than we need to, we give people the wrong message (that we are unconcerned about their problems because we have more important things to rush off and deal with) and we undermine our own morale and energy levels. These problems then create additional pressures and tensions which, in turn, make us feel overburdened and unable to find the time or space to be reflective and get a grip on our workload. Once such a vicious circle has been established it can be very difficult to break out of, even gathering momentum over time and therefore getting worse, with a very real risk of the individual concerned experiencing a significant level of stress.

It is therefore important that we take whatever steps are necessary to create the time and space for personal reflection. This will include seeking support from whatever appropriate quarters we can and making the best use of it. It also involves having faith in our own ability and a commitment to the value of reflective practice.

There are skills and techniques that can be drawn upon to help us manage work pressures as effectively as possible (see the *Guide to Further Learning* at the end of the book). Unfortunately, many professionals have not had the opportunity to learn about such matters, as it is not uncommon for professional education across the helping professions to provide little or no input relating to the knowledge and skills involved in time and workload management. It is as if it is being assumed that, by throwing people in at the deep end of workload pressures, they will learn to swim. Of course, the reality is that some people learn to swim, but perhaps very badly and inefficiently, while others sadly learn how to drown (hence the very high levels of stress in the contemporary workplace). A more sophisticated approach that pays serious attention to these issues is called for in the longer term, but in the meantime individual practitioners and managers would do well to explore the literature on managing work pressures and undertake relevant training where possible (although it has to be said that a significant proportion of the training on 'time management' that is available is of a simplistic nature that does not do justice to the complexities involved).

Self-awareness

It is very easy, especially in highly pressurized work environments, to concentrate on the job at hand and lose sight of our own role in the process. The point was made earlier that reflexive practice, which can be seen as part of the broader enterprise of critically reflective practice, involves becoming more aware of our own role in the circumstances we deal with – in effect, becoming more self-aware.

It is important to recognize that, in the 'people' professions in general (including human resources, for example) and the helping professions in particular, we work with people. This means that self-awareness is an essential component. This is because self-awareness contains two elements that can be summarized in the following two sets of questions:

■ What impact am I having on this situation? How are my role, my personality, my values and my actions and attitudes playing a part in shaping what is happening?

■ What impact is the situation having on me? Are there any aspects I feel uncomfortable about? If so, how is this affecting the situation?

Addressing these questions can be a significant part of creating and using personal reflective space. It is therefore important to make sure that issues of self-awareness are on our personal development agenda.

Taylor recognizes that having courage must be part of this: 'You need courage to look at yourself and your practice because it takes honesty and frankness to move outside your comfort zones' (2006, p. 49). This captures well an important aspect of self-awareness – being prepared to look critically at our own contribution and reflect on how we can not only improve it, but actually maximize our potential. This may involve, as Taylor acknowledges, moving outside our comfort zones – that is, being willing to take reasonable risks in venturing outside what we would normally do or how we would normally think. And that is precisely about courage.

Self-awareness can be developed through receiving feedback from trusted individuals, especially through mentoring, coaching or supervision (see below). However, we can also develop our awareness on our own by looking carefully at what we are doing (or what we have done or plan to do), why we have chosen to move in a particular direction, how we felt about the circumstances, *why* we feel like that, what impact those feelings are having on us, and so on. This is not a recipe for navel gazing that leaves us no time for actual practice. Rather, it is an argument for taking the opportunity from time to time to review our practice, our reactions to the challenges our practice presents us with and how we feel about all this.

In taking forward such opportunities for developing self-awareness, we can become:

■ More aware of the strengths we can build on and the areas for development that we need to work on.

■ More confident in our own abilities through a greater knowledge of what we have to offer.

■ Less likely to drift and 'lose the plot' about what we are doing, however busy we may become.

■ Less likely to become stressed as we will be in a better position to monitor the pressures we are under and recognize when remedial actions need to be taken to prevent pressures overspilling into harmful stress.

It should be clear, then, that using personal reflective space to develop self-awareness (and using self-awareness to create personal reflective space) is well worth the effort.

Being a free thinker

There is a strand in philosophical thought stretching back to the work of Friedrich Nietzsche in the nineteenth century that is critical of the tendency for people to meekly do what is expected of them and follow routines and patterns uncritically, without putting their own stamp on their actions and thus on their lives more broadly. Heller describes Nietzsche as: 'a man who so ferociously fought what had been handed down by the past, diluted as it was by routine and the enfeebled spirit' (1988, p. 174).

Nietzsche's work, and the school of existentialist thought that it in large part inspired, incorporates the important notion of being a 'free spirit' – that is, of not being bound by a mindless acceptance of convention, habit, routine and social pressures. This is clearly very consistent with the philosophy of critically reflective practice. What is also clear is that being a free spirit needs to incorporate being a free thinker – we cannot have the former without the latter.

In terms of personal reflective space, then, becoming a critically reflective practitioner involves using opportunities to forge our own ways forward.

While we may get helpful guidance from others, we also need to look at what is the distinctive contribution we can each make to the work that we do within the helping professions. This is not about being a 'maverick' and ploughing our own furrow, come what may. It is about recognizing that we can make a much more valuable (and rewarding) contribution if we bring a distinctive edge to the situation, if we are imaginative and creative and not simply interested in following routines and set patterns and offering standardized responses. Being a free thinker does not mean that 'anything goes', but it does mean that we can build up our skills in using the 'artistry' of which Schön wrote.

How, then, can we be free thinkers, creative professionals rather than convention-bound bureaucrats? Well, if we were to offer detailed guidance on this, we would be contradicting the whole notion of being a free thinker! What is much more important is for you to give your full attention to developing a positive, creative approach to the problems you encounter in your professional practice rather than looking for formulaic solutions, There are various tools available that can be drawn upon, and adapted where necessary, and put to good use in developing creative approaches (see Chapter 4 for a more detailed discussion of such tools and techniques).

Practice focus 3.1

Simon had got to the point where his work was largely of a routine nature. He had lost his initial enthusiasm and was now experienced enough to deal with most situations in a fairly straightforward way. However, the more routinized his work became, the less satisfying it was and he was now bored with his working life. This prompted him to think about doing an evening class – to give him something interesting and stimulating to do to balance out what had become a boring job.

He had been quite interested in philosophy when he was at university, but he never had a chance to study it in any depth. He therefore welcomed the opportunity to register for a philosophy evening class at his local adult education centre. On the evening they discussed Nietzsche's philosophy in general and the idea of being a free spirit in particular, he began to realize that this is where he had gone wrong. He had allowed himself to get into a situation where he had failed to 'stay fresh' in what he was doing; he had allowed himself to develop a set of 'tramlines' in his work by doing everything in a routine, unthinking way. He had lost sight of the values and commitment that had brought him into the helping professions in the first place. No wonder, he reflected, his work had become so boring and unsatisfying. He therefore started to think about how he could adopt a more free-spirited approach to his work so that it would not be so unstimulating. He also recognized that he would probably be more effective in his work if he were less bored and disillusioned.

Helicopter vision

Butt helps us to understand that: 'Understanding properly involves what Dilthey (1988) saw as a "hermeneutic circle": moving from part to whole and back to part again in order to see how things fit together' (2004, p. 19). This is similar to: (i) the 'part/whole analysis' that Scheff (1997) writes of – that is, the idea that parts need to be understood in relation to wholes and vice versa; and (ii) dialectical thinking, as discussed in Chapter 2. What it boils down to is the importance of having an idea of how specific issues fit into the 'big picture'.

This is where the idea of 'helicopter vision' can be very useful. It refers to the ability to: (i) rise above a situation to get the overview of how the component parts fit together and how they create the overall situation; and (ii) descend back into it to be able to deal with it in an informed way. This is quite a skill, as it is relatively easy to get bogged down in the details of a situation and not have that broader, more holistic view. This means that we can easily be working on the basis of a partial, distorted picture and thus be missing out on some key information, understandings and insights.

Sometimes, having that broader picture or overview can be immensely helpful. In some circumstances, it may be all that is needed. For example, we may have a situation where someone is grieving but does not realize that this is what is happening (see the discussion of grief in Chapter 2), in which we are able to help that person understand what they are going through as part of a broader picture of mourning a loss. Gaining this insight may be enough for that individual to feel more in control of the situation (now that they understand what is happening) and thus confident enough to deal with it without the need for professional intervention.

Helicopter vision is a useful basis for personal reflective space. It can be used as a way of forming a view of the overall picture so that we can reflect on what our role needs to be in general and what specific steps we need to take. It is our experience that, when our practice is unproductive (or even counterproductive), it is often because the practitioner concerned did not have an overview of the situation he or she was dealing with.

Creating the space from time to time to develop a meaningful overview of not only the specific situations we are dealing with, but also our workload and duties as a whole is therefore an important skill to develop. It is a very worthwhile use of our time. This reinforces the point made in Chapter 1 that, the busier we are, the more reflective we need to be. If we do not create the space to gain the overview we need to form an adequate understanding of the situations we are dealing with, then we make our jobs much more difficult, we make our practice much less effective and rewarding, and we contribute to a sense of powerlessness and lack of control and thus to our own demoralization.

Clarity and focus

Busy people run the risk of 'losing the plot', of becoming so busy and distracted that they lose sight of what they are doing and why they are doing it. Extremely busy people run a very significant risk of doing so. It is therefore important that we have sufficient presence of mind to make sure that we retain a clear focus on what we are doing. The discussion of systematic practice in Chapter 4 will help to give a clear picture of how this can be done. Systematic practice can be a useful framework for making sure we are not drifting away from what we are supposed to be doing.

Part of maintaining clarity of focus is to make sure that we have clear goals to aim for, and that these are shared goals, so that everyone involved can be pulling in the same direction (see the discussion of partnership in Chapter 2). If we are not clear about (and focused on) our goals, we are really going to struggle to achieve them. A key part of goal setting is 'problem setting' (or 'problem posing' as it is also known). Schön too emphasizes the importance of problem setting:

> But with this emphasis on problem solving, we ignore problem *setting*, the process by which we define the decision to be made, the ends to be achieved, the means which may be chosen. In real-world practice, problems do not present themselves to the practitioner as givens. They must be constructed from the materials of problematic situations which are puzzling, troubling and uncertain. In order to convert a problematic situation to a problem, a practitioner must do a certain kind of work. He [*sic*] must make sense of an uncertain situation that initially makes no sense.
>
> (1983, p. 40)

This passage captures well the spirit of reflective practice. The problems we face in the helping professions are not 'given', they are not a finite set of distinct situations we label as 'problematic'. Situations have to come to be defined as *problematic* in some way, and when this happens, then it would be wise for it to be based on an informed approach, having carefully considered the situation. If not, we run the risk of wasting valuable resources on situations that are unnecessarily seen as problematic, then we do ourselves, our employers and – most of all – the people we serve a major disservice.

Personal reflective space can therefore be put to good use in making sure that we have clarity and focus, even (or *especially*) when we are under considerable pressure. It may involve a certain amount of our time to establish and maintain such clarity and focus, but that will be nothing compared with how much time, effort and energy will be lost if we lose our focus and lack clarity about what we are doing, how and why we are doing it. The key, then, is the effective (reflective) use of our time – using time to save time and prevent a lack of focus from costing us time (and thus energy and, indirectly, morale).

DYADIC REFLECTIVE SPACE

There is much that a determined and committed individual can do to develop their own critically reflective practice by making the best of personal reflective space, as outlined in the previous section. However, this can also be supplemented by the benefits to be gained from what Clutterbuck (1998) calls 'dyadic reflective space' – that is, opportunities for reflection in pairs. This would include supervision, coaching and mentoring. Our focus, here, then is on how such one-to-one interactions can be used to maximize the potential for, and of, critically reflective practice. We shall explore four aspects of this, beginning with a discussion of the role of experience in learning.

Experience is not the best teacher

It is commonly said that experience is the best teacher. However, in reality this is not actually the case. For example, consider how many people there are who have a lot of experience, but have actually learned little or nothing from it. Experience creates the potential for learning but, in itself, it teaches us nothing directly. It is what we *do with* experience that is the best teacher. The experience provides a basis for learning, but experience alone is not enough. That experience has to be 'processed' – that is, it needs to be translated into actual learning. We can do that ourselves to a certain extent – for example, through personal reflective space, as discussed above. However, what can be especially helpful is when we have the benefit of the support of a skilled and experienced learning facilitator (supervisor, mentor, practice teacher, tutor or coach). Such a facilitator should be able to play a proactive role in helping us identify the learning points to be gleaned from our experience, to facilitate drawing out whatever lessons could be learned from it – not least the following:

- Any mistakes we may have made and how we might avoid these in future.
- What we had done well so that we can build on our successes.
- What knowledge we used and whether it stood the test of being put into practice.
- What gaps there may be in our knowledge base that we will need to work on.
- What skills we used well so that we can make the most of them in future.
- What gaps in our skills that may have become apparent so that we can try to boost our skills in appropriate ways.
- Whether what we did was consistent with our values and, if not, what we would need to do differently next time

The question of finding time for reflection also arises in relation to dyadic reflective space. Drawing out the learning from experience will inevitably involve a time cost for both the learner and the learning facilitator. However, Clutterbuck again makes an important point when he argues that:

> facilitators of learning *create* the time, both for themselves and for others in the team, to support each other in their learning. They often do so in spite of severe practical difficulties.
>
> (1998, p. 14)

A skilled learning facilitator will recognize the importance of dyadic reflective space and will do a good enough time management job of making this aspect of their role a priority.

Voice of experience 3.1

When I joined the team I found my supervisor a bit daunting. She took far more interest in my work than any of my previous line managers. It felt a bit intrusive to begin with, but I soon realized that she was helping me to learn a great deal. She kept asking me why I had done things in a particular way, what my reasoning was and so on. But she also helped me draw out from what I had done ideas about what I might do differently next time, what lessons I might learn from the case. Now it's quite clear to me that I am learning far more here than I ever did in any of my previous jobs. It's great.

Sheila, a specialist child protection health visitor

You are not alone

While there is much to be gained from making effective use of personal reflective space, some people struggle to do it. They need someone else to 'bounce ideas off'. As Harris comments:

> While some professionals have the capacity for unsupported reflection, the majority will require some form of assistance. Similarly, while some professionals learn from every experience, others learn from selective experiences which possess certain characteristics or features.
>
> (1996, p. 37)

It needs to be remembered, then, that there is no shame in feeling that we need help in order to be able to benefit from reflection. Potentially there are many ways in which we can benefit from other people's support:

- **Line management support.** Many managers can be extremely skilful learning facilitators, able to use supervision to excellent effect in promoting reflection (see below).
- **Clinical supervision.** Some professionals receive supervision separate from the line management role. This too has the potential for generating a dialogue that can promote learning and reflection.
- **Mentoring.** Increasingly these days mentoring is being used as an aid to learning and to promoting high-quality professional practice. For those

fortunate enough to have the support of a skilled mentor to draw on, there will be much to be gained.

■ **Coaching.** While mentoring is concerned with learning and development more broadly, coaching tends to be more specific, focusing on specific issues, perhaps for a fixed period of time. It offers great potential for making good use of dyadic reflective space.

■ **Practice teaching/field supervision.** Students in some professional disciplines will be assigned a practice teacher or field supervisor for the duration of their work placement. Promoting reflective practice is a key function of this role.

■ **Tutorials.** Students can benefit from one-to-one tutorials where these are available, as they can provide fertile ground for exploring key ideas and links between theory and practice.

■ **Peer support.** Sometimes there are formal 'pairing' systems in place where individual colleagues are encouraged to support each other and help each other learn (these are sometimes referred to as 'buddy' systems). In addition, informal support systems can often develop whereby colleagues will run ideas by one another and support each other in making sense of the complex issues they face.

In principle, then, there are plenty of opportunities for making use of dyadic reflective space or one-to-one reflection. If in reality, however, you find that you are not having such support (or the support you receive is of poor quality), then it would be wise to explore other possibilities, as you will otherwise be losing out a great deal. While it may be disappointing when learning support systems that should be in place are not, we should none the less not allow the absence of such support to disadvantage us. We should not allow the absence of formal support to discourage us from drawing on informal support if that is all that is available to us.

The role of the line manager

In the current terminology people are 'human resources'. Some people object to this term as they feel that it is dehumanizing to see people as a resource. However, the positive side of this terminology is that it allows us to see that managers have a responsibility to maximize the potential of the people they supervise (in the same way that managers have a duty to make the best use of any resources they have within their area of responsibility). Part of this process of making the best use of the human resources available to an organization is helping people learn – aiming to get the best level of practice possible by investing in staff development. Supervision can be central to this.

Clutterbuck's comments are again helpful:

> The reality today is that the line manager increasingly needs to be a *facilitator* of learning. This is a very different role from team coach, although team coach may be part of it. The facilitator of learning creates *the climate, in which the maximum relevant learning can take place.*
>
> (1998, p. 3)

This passage is doubly significant. On the one hand, one-to-one opportunities to facilitate learning can be extremely valuable, as the supervisor can help to draw out the learning points in a positive and constructive way. On the other hand, line managers, as holders of leadership responsibilities, have a critical role to play in shaping the organizational culture in ways that are supportive of learning and reflection.

Line managers can make good use of supervision to promote best practice. This can be done by:

■ *Building on* existing strengths – making the most of them, extending them as far as possible; and

■ *Building up* areas that are in need of development – sorting out gaps in knowledge and/or skills, working towards turning weaknesses into strengths.

Good supervisors, then, will be well versed in building on and building up, as these are vitally important parts of the supervisory role. Encouraging and supporting reflective practice will, in turn, be important underpinnings of these supervisory activities.

We shall discuss training courses and related matters below, but one important point to note at this point is that supervisors have an important part to play in maximizing the learning to be gained from such activities – for example, by using supervision as an opportunity to prepare for training and to draw out the key learning points after the event by making explicit the links between course activities and discussions and actual practice situations.

However, despite all the good that supervisors can do, line managers can also unfortunately be unhelpful when it comes to promoting learning and reflection. As Clutterbuck comments:

> Much more insidious – and more common – is the manager who has largely given up on his or her own continued learning and for whom helping others to learn is a chore. The opportunity to learn from direct reports, peers and other people has few attractions to such managers – they can't see the point.
>
> (1998, p. 14)

This can be a significant barrier to progress (see the discussion of obstacles to reflective practice in Chapter 6). If you find yourself in such a situation, with a line manager who is not supportive of your learning, then at the very least you will need to think carefully about who else can support your learning (rather than simply accepting that you have to do without learning support), and you may also need to consider whether you need to start looking for employment in a more supportive and reflective setting. Obviously, such decisions should not be taken lightly, but significant damage can be done to our learning, our quality of practice and our morale in the short term and our careers in the long run if we allow ourselves to remain in a non-supportive environment for too long.

Preventing drift

Supervisors, mentors, coaches or others involved in making use of dyadic reflective space are in a very strong position to help prevent or remedy 'drift'. By drift we mean the tendency referred to earlier to become distracted and 'lose the plot' when we are busy or otherwise under pressure. Critically reflective practice can help us to make sure that we remain focused and are clear about what outcomes we are working towards. Effective supervision can be extremely important in monitoring working practices and making sure that they are suitably focused, and helping the practitioner to refocus if drift has set in. This can be done by the supervisor asking on a fairly regular basis what the goals are that the practitioner is working towards in a particular case or situation. It is important that these goals are expressed in a clear and focused way – that is, that they are not so vague as to be unhelpful.

One of the ways in which a supervisor can help to prevent drift is through establishing – and maintaining – clarity about goals. Schön's idea of problem setting is therefore also relevant here: 'Problem setting is a process in which, interactively, we *name* the things to which we will attend and *frame* the context in which we will attend to them' (1983, p. 40). People in supervisory or supportive roles can clearly play an important part in making sure that goals are named (that is, explicitly identified) and the context in which they are to be met is clarified – in other words, a plan will be developed for meeting those goals. Busy practitioners, as we noted earlier, can easily lose focus, and so dyadic reflective space can be put to good use in counteracting this.

Practice focus 3.2

When Ashleigh became Kevin's mentor, she quickly realized that he had a problem with staying focused. He was a very enthusiastic staff member, but he often allowed his enthusiasm to run away with him. This took the form of carrying out his duties without giving adequate thought to what he was doing or why he was doing it. It was as if he felt that his commitment to doing a good job would be enough on its own. Ashleigh therefore recognized that, if he was going to be able to learn and develop over time, she was going to have to get him to be much more reflective about what he was trying to achieve – what he saw as his goals in each of the pieces of work he was involved with. To begin with she saw this as a daunting challenge, but she was very pleasantly surprised at how responsive Kevin was once she started talking to him about the importance of goal setting. This helped her to realize just how powerful and helpful a tool mentoring can be in promoting reflective practice. She could see the value of what, on her mentoring course, had been referred to as 'dyadic reflective space'.

GROUP REFLECTIVE SPACE

In addition to solo and one-to-one opportunities for reflection, we also have group opportunities to consider, and these are precisely what we explore in this section – those situations where people have scope for reflecting and learning alongside others in a group setting.

Group learning opportunities

There are various group learning possibilities that can offer useful opportunities for reflection and therefore for learning, development and the enhancement of practice. The main ones are:

- **Training courses**. In-service training courses and workshops can offer excellent opportunities for debate, discussion and exploration of key practice issues, blending theory and practice and thus providing a platform for learning and development.
- **Conferences and seminars**. Although often more formal than training courses, conferences and seminars can none the less offer valuable group learning opportunities.
- **Learning sets**. Some organizations invite interested parties to form a 'learning set' about a particular issue or set of issues (the introduction of a new policy, for example, or a particular aspect of practice that is causing concern). The group will meet for a set amount of time over an agreed period of time to explore the topic in question and seek to use the opportunity (the group reflective space created) to learn about the subject matter and consider how best to take it forward. Learning sets are not simply policy planning or service development groups (see below), as their primary focus is on learning.
- **Team events**. Extended team meetings devoted to professional development and team 'awaydays' can provide excellent opportunities for group reflective space. They allow a set of colleagues to review working practices, the underlying values and philosophy and future developments.
- **Service development groups**. While the primary focus of such groups or 'working parties' is on *service* development, a useful by-product of working as part of such a group is that much personal and professional development can also be achieved as a result of the opportunity for a group of professionals to reflect on aspects of their working systems and practices.

In principle, then, there should be no shortage of opportunities to work in groups to promote one another's understanding of the work challenges we face. These can be an excellent source of learning, new ideas and insights and can also be very useful for confidence building.

Group reflective learning opportunities can help us to take our thinking forward by exploring ideas together and seeing how other people address issues. Gould's comments are significant in this regard:

> reflective learning recognizes that a purpose of education is to facilitate people as (in Bateson's terms) double-loop learners who are able to challenge the normative context of practice, and to be non-defensive and adaptive learners within a constantly evolving professional environment (Bateson, 1973).
>
> (1996, p. 5)

Double-loop learners are those who learn how to learn – that is, who become self-directed learners who are able to deduce principles from their experience that can be applied to new situations. Senge (1994), referring to the work of Argyris and Schön (1978), points out that single-loop learners adjust their behaviour to suit fixed goals, norms and assumptions, while double-loop learners are involved in reviewing and, where appropriate, renegotiating those goals, norms and assumptions. Double-loop learners, as Gould indicates, are therefore better suited to dealing with changing professional environments. Group reflective space can be very useful for promoting double-loop learning, because it offers a variety of perspectives and thus the potential for broadening our outlook on how we tackle the issues involved. It can give us greater flexibility through having the opportunity to see a range of different responses to the same issues and, to a certain extent, can give us greater confidence in moving away from our established habits and preferred ways of working.

Voice of experience 3.2

I was a bit anxious when I was asked to join a 'learning set'; I wasn't really sure what to expect. But I'm really glad I joined. I met people who had a very different take on the situation. Being able to see the situation from different perspectives really opened up new possibilities for me. It made me realize that I have always tended to be quite conservative in my thinking, not really keen to explore different ways of understanding the situation or how to deal with it. It did me a lot of good.

Ronnie, an early years worker

Dimensions of learning

Group learning experiences, such as training courses, are not simply opportunities to learn new knowledge, to be filled up like a container. Knowledge development is part of what is involved in such events, especially where there is a need for new knowledge as a result of a change in the law or policy. However, a fuller picture would include other dimensions of group learning, such as the following:

■ **Developing skills.** Learning about – and perhaps even practising – new skills can be a very worthwhile part of such activities. Having the opportunity to learn about how other participants use their skills can also be invaluable.

■ **Developing values.** Developing a fuller picture of the values underpinning our work in the helping professions can be a very worthwhile pursuit, especially where there is the opportunity to explore value conflicts, moral dilemmas and some of the other complexities that can arise in relation to professional values.

■ **Boosting confidence.** Reflecting together and learning together can be a very important source of confidence. Realizing that other people have anxieties too can make us feel better about our own limitations and concerns – it can help put things in perspective.

■ **Affirmation, validation and consolidation.** Reaffirming our existing knowledge, skills and values can be an important function of group activities. Having the chance to be reminded about how extensive and important our knowledge base is, how wide ranging and significant our skills base is can be a very reassuring and helpful experience. In addition, revisiting our value base can be very affirming and even inspiring at times.

These are not the only ones but should be enough to show how varied group learning and reflection can be in terms of the functions it fulfils, the benefits it brings. Having this broader understanding can help us to appreciate the value of such group reflection opportunities and can perhaps help prepare us for making the most of such opportunities as and when they arise – as well as perhaps encouraging us to seek out or even create opportunities.

Making the most of opportunities

Achieving maximum benefits from group reflection situations can be divided into three parts; before, during and after:

- **Before.** Thinking ahead to try and anticipate what learning opportunities will arise can be of considerable benefit. For example, in advance of a training course, it can be very fruitful to look at the learning objectives for the course and consider how you can best prepare for the experience (perhaps by doing some pre-course reading on the subject or discussing the issues with your line manager or mentor). Those people who arrive at a course, having given the course subject matter no thought whatsoever are likely to get far less out of the course than somebody who is already 'tuned in' to the issues that are likely to be covered.

- **During.** This is a good opportunity for reflection-in-action – being able to concentrate carefully and focus on making the best of the situation while it is happening. Part of this is recognizing our own responsibility for learning and being proactive in seeking out the learning that can be gained. For example, there is much to be gained from trying to identify explicit learning points from the course activities and discussions. This involves using our analytical skills to make sense of the experience and relate the discussion points to our work roles. This is far more likely to produce valuable learning than taking a passive approach that involves sitting back and waiting to be 'enlightened' by the trainer.

- **After.** This relates to what is referred to as the 'transfer of learning' (that is, transferring insights from the course to our own practice settings). It links in with the discussion of 'transfer of learning' below and is also relevant to our earlier discussion about how supervision can be important in drawing out the learning from group learning activities.

What all three of these have in common is an emphasis on an active approach to learning, one in which we take responsibility for maximizing the benefits we can gain from the experience. It is unfortunately the case that many people have had an experience of the education system that has left them with a passive approach to learning – an expectation that others (teachers, tutors, trainers) will fill them with knowledge (what Freire, 1972, refers to as banking model of education: 'depositing' knowledge in relatively empty vessels). It does not take much to work out that this is not consistent with the philosophy of critically reflective practice. In place of such a passive approach, we need to have an understanding of education, training and other group reflection opportunities that is more to do with actively seeking out the learning available – taking a professional approach to using group reflective space positively and proactively.

Transfer of learning

For many years now, a recurring question in the world of education and training has been: how do we make sure that the learning that takes place in the classroom or training venue gets transferred to the actual world of practice? This is recognized as an important issue, as it is so easy for someone to return to their place of work and quickly become immersed in their day-to-day pressures and soon lose sight of whatever benefits they were able to glean from the classroom experience (or other group learning experience). Given that this danger is such an ever-present possibility, it is very wise to guard against it. This can be achieved, in part at least, by:

- Leaving the event with a clear action plan of what key points arising from it will need to be put into practice and how this will be done (or, if there is no time during the actual event, establishing such an action plan as soon as possible thereafter).
- Discussing such an action plan in supervision and obtaining support in making it a reality.
- Reviewing the action plan from time to time to make sure it is being implemented and has not been allowed to slip off the agenda.

This may sound as though it involves a lot of effort, but it need not do so as, once it becomes an established habit, it need not take up much of our time. Also, given the significant positive potential of this approach (and the great waste of effort if it is not adopted), then any such investment of time and effort will be handsomely repaid.

Benner, Hooper-Kyriakidis and Stannard makes an important point (relating specifically to nursing but applicable to the helping professions as a whole):

We are alarmed by the discouragement and demoralization of nurses who are asked to do more than is possible and who are not given the time to do their caregiving work. When nurses are not given the time to be attentive, the large-scale health systems we have created become dangerous places.

(1999, p. 22)

This shows how unrealistic expectations of staff can be not only problematic in terms of the potential for creating stress, but also as a barrier to transferring learning. People who return from a group event to an over-pressurized work setting will find it difficult to make a successful transfer of learning – ironically, then wasting the precious time they invested in the actual event. This brings us back to our discussion in Chapter 1 of the importance of recognizing that the busier we are, the more reflective we need to be. We can now add: the busier we are, the more important it is to make sure that precious time devoted to training or other such events is not wasted as a result of the learning not being transferred.

Gould is correct in stating that: 'There is always a danger that a concept such as reflective learning will become little more than a slogan' (1996, p. 2). We should therefore make sure that we do not allow difficulties in transfer of learning to add to this. The use of group reflective space becomes tokenistic if there is no real payoff in terms of transfer of learning.

Practice focus 3.3

Rachid had attended several in-service training courses since taking up his post after leaving university. They had all been reasonably enjoyable and stimulating events that he thought would be useful. However, something that happened on another course made him wonder just how useful (or otherwise) the previous training had been. Towards the end of this particular course, he was asked to work with a partner to review what had been learned from the day and what they might do differently in their practice in future as a result of the course. In introducing the exercise, the training facilitator commented that a lot of training is a waste of time because, no matter how hard the participants work and how interesting they find the discussions, so many people go back to work after the course and fail to implement any of the learning. The trainer used the term 'magical thinking' to describe this – assuming that, by having these discussions and going through the exercises, this would automatically make them better at their jobs. This trainer pointed out the naivety of this assumption and argued that, if we do not have clarity about how we are going to behave differently or bear different things in mind, then there is a danger that no real learning will have taken place. This made Rachid realize that, although he had worked hard on previous courses, he wasn't able to identify a single, specific way his practice had improved as a result of attending. He realized now that he would have to be more proactive in transferring the training-room learning into his actual work, to make sure that he saw the process through. He knew now it would not happen 'by magic'.

CONCLUSION

Critically reflective practice involves, by its nature as a holistic approach (that is, one that appreciates the 'big picture'), developing a sensitivity to contextual factors. This chapter has emphasized the significance of context by clarifying, as far as we reasonably can in the space available, how the personal, dyadic and group contexts of reflection can be very significant. We would argue that developing a good understanding of these issues is an essential prerequisite for maximizing the potential of reflective practice. We have therefore presented what we see as a sound foundation for understanding the basics and for developing our understanding further. In doing so, we have shown how important it is to be sensitive to the different contexts for reflection and the different approaches that are needed for each, while also identifying, to a certain extent, at least, what these different contexts have in common.

Part 2

Making Reflective Practice a Reality

Chapter 4

Using Strategies and Techniques

INTRODUCTION

Developing reflective practice is not something that can be done by adopting set formulas or following instructions – it is a much more creative, variable and complex undertaking than that. There are, however, strategies and techniques that can be drawn upon to help us develop critically reflective practice, both our own and that of others (if we are supervisors, mentors or practice teachers, for example).

The 'toolbox' of potential techniques we can draw upon is quite immense. For that reason, we have selected a range that relates to each of the three aspects of reflective practice described in Chapter 1, namely:

- Reflection-for-action
- Reflection-in-action
- Reflection-on-action

For each of these three aspects we shall highlight approaches that are: (i) question based; (ii) empowerment based; and (iii) geared towards problem solving. Please note that, while we have chosen to associate particular techniques with either reflection-for-action, reflection-in-action or reflection-on-action, some of the tools presented can apply to more than one of these categories, and so we would urge you to use them flexibly and creatively to suit the circumstances you are dealing with.

Before reading about these various tools or techniques, you may find it helpful to reread the explanation of the three forms of reflection in Chapter 1.

Our intention in choosing these is merely to try to give you a flavour of what is already out there, of what other people in similar circumstances to you have found helpful and to underline the point that reflective practice is not just about what we do, but also how and why we do it. You may find these particular strategies and techniques more or less useful, depending on the circumstances in which you are working and on your preferred styles of working. If these particular tools are not especially helpful to you, then what is important is that they inspire you to go on to find techniques that you do find helpful.

What works for one person will not necessarily work for another. For example, some people find reflective techniques that rely on a predefined set of questions restrictive, while others find the focus they bring helps them to get a good overview of the situation. Furthermore, some approaches are particularly useful for those times when we are reflecting on our own (personal reflective space), while others can be more helpful when we are bouncing ideas off someone else (dyadic reflective space) or in a group reflective space context.

Whether you are concerned with developing your own practice or with promoting and/or assessing critically reflective practice in others, the techniques and approaches that follow have the potential to prove useful for both. We hope that they inspire you to adopt, adapt or design others for your own purposes.

Please note that some of these tools are based on work previously undertaken by one of the present authors – see Thompson (2006b).

TOOLS FOR PROMOTING REFLECTION

1 Reflection-for-action: question-based techniques

1.1 Systematic practice
This is an approach to practice that requires us to focus on three questions when we first start planning any form of intervention. Their purpose is to help prevent 'drift' – that feeling of not really being able to keep a handle on what we are doing and why we are doing it, and of not being able to justify our courses of action if required to do so. Thompson's (2002) model of systematic practice is based around three key questions. These are:

■ **What are you trying to achieve?** This question asks us to identify aims and objectives, and is therefore concerned with goal setting.

■ **How are you going to achieve it?** This second question is about the processes involved in getting us from where we are now to where we want to be. So, if the first question is about goal setting, then the second is about strategy setting.

■ **How will you know when you have achieved it?** One of the strengths of this framework is that the third question acts as a check on our proposals for action, helping to ensure that our goals are achievable and our strategies appropriate.

The first two questions are commonly used as part of planning and assessment. However, the third question is often omitted, even though it can be crucial in ensuring that we have answered the first two questions appropriately and have not been too vague in doing so. For example, if the answer given to the first question was: 'To improve the relationship between Mr Barnes and his daughter', and to the second: 'By arranging for them to go out for a meal together once a week after school', then the third question highlights a potential problem. How would we know that the relationship had improved? Improved to what extent? Would we be able to judge when it was appropriate to withdraw from the situation? Would we know what success looked like in this case?

Systematic practice is about having a plan, albeit one that can be revisited and revised, rather than fumbling about in the dark, hoping that things will work out if we try long and hard enough. But that plan needs to be workable or else it will not provide the structure needed to prevent 'drift'.

The apparent simplicity of this framework of questions belies its usefulness. The questions are short and easy to remember, but many students, practitioners and managers have found them invaluable in terms of being able to feel in control of their workload and earning the professional credibility that comes along with being focused.

Voice of experience 1.2

I've been on a couple of training courses where I've heard about techniques that sound really useful and I fully intend to try them out, but then I tend to fall back into my usual work patterns once I get back to the office. This time, though, someone introduced me to a framework that had the potential to address my biggest failing – keeping a focus on aims and objectives without getting sidetracked and losing the plot. When I got back to the office I printed out the key questions that this approach suggests we focus on and pinned the page to the wall opposite my desk. Using this framework has helped me to develop new work patterns, as it has become my starting point for analysing what I'm planning to do. In fact it's worked so well that I've been tempted to take the notice down, but, I think I'll leave it there as a talking point.

Josie, a care manager

1.2 Objectives tree

Many people find a visual representation of plans and ideas easier to work with than verbal discussion or lines of prose. If you are one of those people, then engaging in reflection-for-action by using a tree diagram to focus your thoughts is something that you might find helpful. While the questions are not dissimilar to those discussed earlier, the difference here is that boxes and inter-linking lines are used to help make thought processes more explicit. As with systematic practice, the first step is to ask the question:

What are you trying to achieve? The aim identified provides the content for the first box at the top of the page (see Figure 4.1). The next step in this technique is to ask:

What it is that will contribute to the achievement of that aim? There are likely to be a number of contributing factors and each one needs to be given its own box in a second tier, all linked by lines to that initial tier. Once these have been identified, a third question needs to be posed:

What action needs to be taken to bring about what has been highlighted in each of the second tier of boxes? As you have probably guessed, these action plans form the content of a third tier of steps to be taken. This process can take a fair bit of time if you are new to it, but it can pay dividends to persevere until you become more familiar with it as a way of working. The fact that there is a visual representation in front of you can help keep your mind focused on what you are trying to achieve, particularly as the box containing the original aim will always be at the forefront, especially if the size of paper used allows for the objectives tree to fit onto one page.

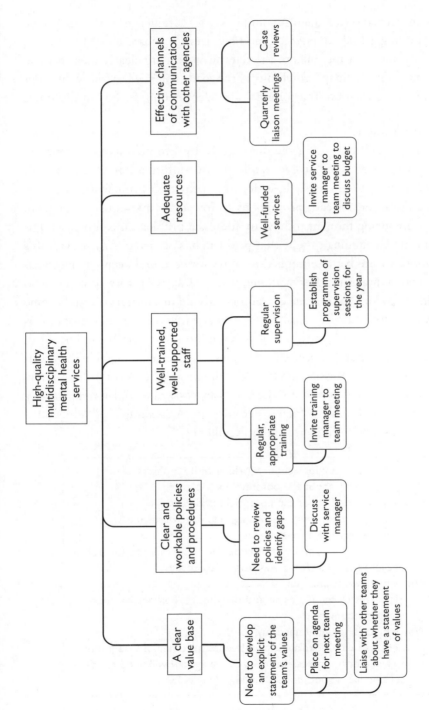

Figure 4.1 Example of an objective line

You can keep the tree diagram simple or, as confidence in the technique grows, you might find yourself adding new tiers, or subsections of tiers. The trick is to ensure that the links to the relevant boxes are clearly identified, so that the outcome is a 'map' which shows the roads you need to follow in order to reach your destination (that original aim identified in the box at tier one).

1.3 Embedded whys

This approach relies on using the question 'Why?' to help us to understand the underlying reasons for problems and provide information which, in turn, will inform our actions. As such, it does not provide a framework of predefined questions but, instead, prompts us to formulate questions of our own. When we are giving thought to how to address a problem, it can be useful to have some understanding of why that problem has occurred. Armed with this information, we are better equipped to move forward and keep any intervention focused and relevant. For example, if we are working with someone who is debilitated by anxiety, then any attempts to build up confidence can become counterproductive if the reasons for the anxiety are not well understood. It is unusual for one 'why?' question to get to the root of any problem, but it can lead us into another and another 'why?' question (each embedded in the previous one like a set of Russian dolls – see Thompson, 2006b) until we really start to uncover what lies at the heart of an issue and understand exactly where our problem-solving focus needs to be. An example of 'embedded whys' giving us a better understanding would be:

> Why am I feeling anxious about working with Mr Walters?
> – I am worried about the potential for violence.
> Why am I worried about the potential for violence?
> – Last time I went there he was aggressive towards me.
> Why was he aggressive towards me?
> – He seemed to think I was intending to report him to the police because I was aware he was using illegal drugs.
> Why would he assume that?
> – He seems to see me as an authority figure. Perhaps he doesn't understand my role.
> Why wouldn't he understand my role?
> – Perhaps I didn't explain it clearly enough to him. If I want him to avoid being aggressive towards me again, I will need to make sure he has a good understanding of my role.

If you are using this technique with others to promote their reflective practice, it needs to be utilized sensitively, as it can feel threatening to be asked 'why?', especially several times over. We would urge you to read more about it if you think you might want to adopt it as a strategy (see Thompson, 2006b). Our purpose here is just to introduce it as an example of how question-based frameworks do not have to be pre-structured in order to be useful.

2 Reflection-for-action: emancipatory techniques

2.1 Visioning

As the name implies this technique is about imagining a future situation. It is included here as an emancipatory technique, because it implies working towards a positive future. For many people in poor health, distress or disadvantage it is often difficult to envisage a positive future, but there are techniques which can help at this stage of reflection-for-action. For example, we can invite people to make their hopes and fears explicit by asking them to imagine what they could wish for if you told them you had acquired a magic wand. Such a technique can help people to bring emotional issues to the surface where they can more easily be addressed. Having a sense of where someone wants to get to in their life can provide the basis for future work with them to that end.

Having a vision of a hoped-for outcome can also foster commitment to proposed forms of action, especially where the necessary steps are likely to prove difficult, as might be the case when someone wants to overcome an addiction, for example. Visioning can also work for us in our roles as members of the helping professions. When we feel demoralized or disempowered, visioning ourselves as confident and competent can help us to discover what we need to do in order to get to that stage and, as such, feed into our continuous professional development.

2.2 If I were . . .

This is a technique which can help us to reflect on our role, and what it is that we can bring to a situation. As such, it can provide a confidence boost by highlighting to ourselves and others the uniqueness of our particular role within multidisciplinary endeavours to bring about change. When reflecting on a way forward, it can be useful to try to put ourselves in the shoes of other people involved in a given situation and to consider what we could contribute if we were in their position. So, for example we might surmise that, '*If I were a physiotherapist*, I would be able to work with Mrs Leeson towards improving her breathing technique and mobility.' Or, '*If I were a housing officer*, I could help to get her rehoused in accommodation that would better suit her need.' Identifying the uniqueness of colleagues' roles and responsibilities can be a useful prompt for reflecting on one's own role and responsibilities – to think about what *we* in our own particular capacity can do to make a positive difference. As well as being a confidence boost, reflecting in this way can help to refine our planning, so that we do not waste time duplicating the work that could be done adequately, or perhaps more competently, by a colleague from another discipline, but concentrate instead on our particular strengths.

Students, and those assessing their progress, may find this a helpful technique for assessing how well they understand the boundaries of their role.

2.3 Chunk up, chunk down

While the previous technique focuses on the power of individuals to contribute to positive change, this one reminds us to consider the wider context within which individuals operate, and can prompt us to consider at what level our intervention might be most effective.

It has its roots in the field of neurolinguistic programming (NLP) and refers to the process of moving between two levels of analysis – broad thinking and narrow. The term 'chunking down' refers to moving away from broader issues to concentrate on finer detail, while 'chunking up' refers to the opposite – moving from fine detail to consider the bigger picture. Those with some knowledge of sociology may recognize these distinctions in the different approaches of sociologists such as Goffman (1971) and other symbolic interactionists who focused on the micro-level interactions between individuals, and Marx (Wheen, 2000) and other structuralist thinkers who focused in the macro level of wider social structures and processes. This is not to say that this technique requires an in-depth understanding of sociology or, indeed, psychology, but it does highlight the need to consider whether 'chunking up' or 'chunking down' might throw light on a situation, or suggest a useful way forward. What needs to be borne in mind, however, is that it is not a matter of *either* a broad *or* a narrow focus – both broad and narrow thinking have their part to play and problems occur when one is used to the exclusion of the other or in the wrong circumstances.

3 Reflection-for-action: problem-solving techniques

3.1 *The RED approach*

This is a tool that was specifically designed to help staff and managers in the 'people professions' to address conflict situations. As such, it can be a valuable aid to reflection-for-action where a calm and focused approach is needed in order to address tension. It is referred to as the RED approach because it has three elements:

> ■ **R** – refers to the need to *recognize* conflict. It is not uncommon for busy practitioners to fail to recognize a situation as one involving conflict and they may mistakenly interpret it in individualistic terms. For example, being in conflict with someone named Sam may be interpreted as 'Sam is being awkward' rather than more realistically perhaps as 'Sam and I are in conflict with one another.'
> ■ **E** – indicates the need to *evaluate* conflict. This means weighing up how significant the conflict is and what is likely to be the best response to it in the circumstances. Some conflicts may be so minor that they may be safely left alone, while others certainly cannot be.
> ■ **D** – stands for *dealing* with conflict. Conflict situations can be very demanding and so thinking carefully about how to handle them is an important part of the process. Entering a conflict situation non-reflectively can make the enterprise more dangerous than it needs to be.

As an approach, it calls on the person dealing with conflict to draw on what he or she knows about feelings, and particularly about heightened emotions, to inform what they do in conflict situations and how they do it. Without this prior reflection, it is all too easy to exacerbate a tense situation and put ourselves and others in unnecessary danger. If our intention is to solve a problem, then adding to it is not going to be a satisfactory outcome! Using the RED approach will not make anyone an expert in dealing with conflict, nor do you have to be a conflict expert in order to use it. Its usefulness is as a reflective tool for thinking things through before 'getting stuck in' and making a difficult situation worse because we have not recognized that it *is* a conflict situation, or taken on board the knowledge base that already exists about handling such situations.

Practice focus 4.1

Jules's first day as practice manager had not been easy. There had been numerous demands on his time from lots of different quarters. By late afternoon he had still not had time for a break and was feeling quite disorientated. When one of the patients insisted on speaking to him about the long waiting times at the health centre, Jules suggested that he 'join the queue'. At this the patient became extremely angry and took several very tense minutes to placate. Jules's initial reaction was to blame the patient for being oversensitive – after all, he had only meant it as a joke. But, after a very welcome cup of coffee and an opportunity to gather his thoughts, he realized that he had been insensitive. When he had made his flippant remark, he had not taken into account that patients at a surgery are likely to be experiencing heightened emotions for one reason or another and that being kept waiting would only have added another to this. This was something he knew about and, with his knowledge of conflict and conflict management, he was surprised that he hadn't seen it coming. As well as knowing about conflict, he had experience of managing it too – in fact, that had helped him to get the job in the first place – but he was disappointed that he hadn't recognized this situation as one and dealt with it more appropriately.

3.2 Cost-benefit analysis

While this is something that can be used at any stage of reflection, this is a very useful planning tool in a number of ways, including:

- establishing a working relationship based on partnership
- promoting trust
- establishing priorities
- highlighting positives.

As an aid to decision making it provides the visual record that many people find useful. The simple process involves drawing a line down the middle of a sheet of paper and heading one side 'Costs' and the other 'Benefits'. It can be used by an individual, but is especially useful for helping someone else in assisting them to 'see the wood for the trees', when their thinking has become muddled. Very often, people who are distressed or anxious find it difficult to make decisions, and so this tool can be helpful by making the consequences of particular courses of action explicit. Few decisions are straightforward, and there is usually some sort of trade off involved. Cost-benefit analysis can help people to project their thinking forward, so that they can envisage the benefits that might result in the future from taking a difficult decision in the present. It also has the great strength of providing a form of informal contract to which we can return if the person we are working with does not feel happy with a decision or course of action, which means that we are less likely to be targeted for blame.

It is also very useful for encouraging reflection about the consequences of decision making from a variety of perspectives – in effect, it can encourage people to put themselves in other people's shoes, which is often helpful where conflict is involved. So, when thinking about the 'costs' element, the question 'the cost to whom?' can be used very effectively to broaden out a person's thinking and remind them of their obligations to others in a given situation.

3.3 Rehearsing

Again, this approach is about projecting into the future and using what is already known about human psychology and social and organizational behaviour to help identify and prepare for problems that we are likely to encounter when embarking on a chosen course, rather than thinking after the event that we might have handled it better. However, it goes beyond predicting likely outcomes and involves actually rehearsing how we might respond to them in a positive way. That is not to say that we need to rehearse whole speeches, although some people do find it useful to have some sort of 'script' in their head, or a list of bullet points on a notepad, in advance of a situation. Anticipating a response or set of behaviours allows for thinking time – drawing on what is known about, for example, likely behaviour in conflict situations or when someone is going to be given bad or unwelcome news. Rehearsing allows us to act out scenarios in our heads, and to revise or reject approaches that do not seem as effective or appropriate as we had first thought.

As well as being a helpful exercise for individual workers when interacting with colleagues, managers and so on, this type of reflection-for-action can be used to good effect with people we are seeking to help who feel unconfident about participating in meetings, addressing conflict situations, or any set of circumstances for which they feel unprepared or powerless. Practice teachers and mentors might also find this works well with students and other learners.

4 Reflection-in-action: question-based approaches

4.1 Risk assessment models

While risk assessment is an important aspect of planning ahead, it is often the case in potentially hazardous situations that we are required to think on our feet – to make decisions while in the midst of the action. The strength of risk models is that they provide a framework for ordering our thoughts when the pressure is on to think and act quickly, especially when vulnerable, confused and sometimes frightened people are looking to us for guidance. It can be reassuring to know that other workers have been in that situation before us, and it makes sense to at least consider the advice of others who have experienced or researched the very difficulties we are facing. For example, Brearley (1982) poses questions which prompt us to think about, amongst other things, what turns a *potentially* risky situation into an *actual* one. Doel and Shardlow (2005) reproduce a risk assessment tool which highlights a number of areas of risk, including financial, social, environmental, psychological, familial and physical risks, which also requires us to explore and evaluate each new situation rather than following well-trodden and routine paths.

There are many risk assessment tools available, and we need to be selective in our usage of them because they do not all do the same job. What should guide us in choosing a risk-assessment framework as a tool for reflection-in-action is whether the questions it poses help us to decide:

- whether to act
- when to act
- whether we have enough information on which to base an informed decision.

4.2 The 3 Hs: Head – Heart – Habit

When in the midst of a difficult situation, it can be all too easy to concentrate on one aspect at the expense of others. Keeping these three words (head, heart and habit) at the forefront of our consciousness can remind us to think about how and why humans behave in the ways that we do – especially what it is that motivates behaviour. Armed with this knowledge, and having taken time out to reflect on it, we become better equipped to facilitate positive change.

These three key words prompt us to ask the questions that can help inform our actions, so that they are not based on routine or guesswork:

> ■ **Head.** What part is reasoning playing here? The brain will be processing ideas and trying to make sense of them in a situation where a decision is required.

- **Heart**. What emotions are involved here (for example fear, excitement, hope) and how are they impacting on behaviour?
- **Habit**. Is this about long-established patterns of behaviour which are continuing because they have never been called into question?

A great deal of time can be spent on producing a plan of action to address a particular issue but, if one or more of the 'Three Hs' is ignored, then the success of that plan may become compromised. For example, in a shared action plan, both helper and person being helped can accept something as 'the right thing to do' at a rational level, but that plan may not come to fruition if something at an emotional level affects motivation – if their heart is not in it, as it were. Furthermore, even where commitment and motivation are present, habits are often hard to break, and plans may well go adrift if the potential for habit to affect behaviour is ignored or underestimated.

4.3 Think–feel–do

This is a similar technique, in that it reminds us about human psychology and the need to consider the different dimensions of human experience: thoughts, feelings and actions. This framework can help us to avoid going into 'automatic pilot mode' where, in the midst of pressure to get things done, the impact of feelings, and the benefits of reflection, tend to get minimized or forgotten altogether. It is not so much a case of providing direct questions in themselves, but rather keywords for basing questions on – questions such as: 'Have I thought this through?'; 'Are the risk factors too high?'; 'Will she be too frightened to move out of this relationship?'; 'Is this the right time?'; and so on. As such, using *Think-Feel-Do* as a kind of mantra can act as a 'reality check' when work pressures are high and remind us that we are people working with people and not robots working with inanimate objects. Even though we might feel more comfortable with one or two of the three aspects, effective practice requires that we address all three.

This framework can be useful for clarifying our own thinking and how our feelings are influencing the situation, but it is also a very valuable tool to be used by people with a responsibility for promoting reflective practice in others (supervisors, mentors or practice teachers, for example).

5 Reflection-in-action: emancipatory approaches

5.1 Reframing

This approach can be very effective for getting people to think of themselves and their situation in a different light. Sometimes progress towards a goal is hampered by a sense of hopelessness or negativity, especially where self-esteem is low. There is something to be said for perseverance, but it can become counterproductive to continue with a course of action when someone is experiencing these feelings, as it tends to set up a vicious circle. For example, failure becomes more likely where there is a tendency for low self-esteem to affect energy and commitment – this feeds back into the low self-esteem and reinforces it. People can then perceive this outcome as a self-fulfilling prophecy and use it to reaffirm their negative self-perception through comments such as: 'I told you I'd never be able to do this', and so on.

Reframing is a technique that can help to turn these feelings around, so that people feel more positive and therefore more likely to succeed in their aims. Imagine, for example, that you have been working with a young woman with a learning disability, hoping that she will gain enough confidence to enrol for a course in fashion design at her local college. If she perceives herself as 'stupid' and the students and tutors as 'clever', then it is unlikely that she will ever feel confident enough to make that step, however much you try to bolster her self-esteem. The strength of the reframing technique is that it requires us to stop and rethink – to take a step back to consider different perspectives and to offer up a different interpretation of events and perceptions, one that puts things in a different and more positive light. So, for example, if the situation with this young woman were to be reframed so that she is persuaded to see herself not as stupid, but as an enthusiastic woman with a vivid imagination and lots of ideas, then a successful outcome is more likely to be achieved.

As a technique, it need not take much time to put into practice, but it has the potential to turn things around dramatically because of the effect it can have on confidence and motivation. It is an example of where thinking 'on our feet', but without falling foul of BOB (the Bypassing Our Brain problem), can make the difference between a negative and a positive self-image.

5.2 Noticing

This is a term used by Boud and Walker (1990) to refer to the need to pay attention to key aspects of the situation. It is based on a recognition of the importance of observational skills – the ability to draw out from our experience those aspects of the situation that are particularly significant. As such, 'noticing' is an important activity when it comes to reflective practice.

However, with specific reference to *critically* reflective practice, as we noted in Chapter 1, Mezirow (1983) introduced a useful approach known as 'perspective transformation'. This involves recognizing constraints that socialization into a particular culture tends to put on our thinking, as well as how we see and value things. Perspective transformation has much in common with reframing, but relates more specifically to the development of *emancipatory* understandings – that is, approaches that challenge the potentially oppressive stereotyping of certain groups (people with mental health problems, for example).

Maximizing our ability for 'noticing' can be a very useful strategy for promoting reflection, both our own and that of others for whom we have a responsibility for encouraging and supporting learning. Where we are able to incorporate perspective transformation, with its emphasis on the empowering potential of freeing people up from constraints, then this is even better.

5.3 Avoiding, or breaking out of, the drama triangle
The helping professions tend to attract people who want to make a difference to other people's lives, but this enthusiasm for offering support and trying to 'make things better' can become problematic if care is not taken to maintain appropriate boundaries when involved in situations of conflict. In such circumstances, people who see themselves as 'victims' of the wrongdoing or insensitivity of others will often be looking for someone to 'rescue' them, and we need to keep our wits about us if we are not to be drawn into conflicts and ascribed a role we did not sign up for, or see as appropriate.

The term 'drama triangle' comes from the field of transactional analysis (see the *Guide to Further Learning* at the end of the book) and helps us to understand the 'space between people' – the processes that take place within group dynamics (Hopkins, 1986). Transactional analysis is too complex an approach to try to explain it adequately in the space we have here, but we have picked out the 'drama triangle' concept as an example of something which can inform our understanding of situations as they unfold.

The drama triangle involves three 'players'.

- **The victim**. This person has a real or imagined understanding that someone is doing them harm, is bringing a threat to their happiness, or is in some way persecuting them.
- **The persecutor**. This person is perceived by the 'victim' as the guilty party, as the person responsible for causing the problems.
- **The rescuer**. This is the person who is seen by the 'victim' as an avenue for addressing the problems caused by the 'persecutor'.

The problem with this triangle is that it involves the development of an unhealthy dynamic. Members of the helping professions can be a prime target for being seen as a 'rescuer' – seduced into taking sides and losing neutrality, perhaps only to find out later that the victim's perception of being persecuted was not an accurate one (it is sometimes the case that it turns out to be the 'victim' who has been doing the persecuting). The drama triangle can lead us to adopt one person's partial interpretation instead of developing our own more holistic, thorough and impartial assessment. Being aware of the dangers of the drama triangle can help us to avoid falling into the trap of being drawn into taking sides.

This provides an important example of where reflection-in-action can make the difference between mindful and mindless practice and thereby empower us as workers and managers – where drawing on research and practice experience can highlight awareness and help prevent our objectivity being compromised.

6 Reflection-in-action: problem-solving approaches

6.1 Using dissonance

In any form of work in the helping professions, we are likely to encounter some degree of opposition to change. A reluctance to explore and perhaps reconsider long-held views and attitudes can become a barrier to change and can help to maintain power imbalances, particularly where the attitudes are discriminatory. 'Cognitive dissonance' describes a state experienced when there is a contradiction between two sets of ideas. We find ourselves in a situation that causes us discomfort and cannot be easily tolerated unless one set of ideas is revised or abandoned. For example, we might have been working with a very experienced mentor for many years and, because we respect his or her judgement, we would normally have made this person our first port of call when looking for advice. One day, we overhear a team colleague that we respect complaining about what they perceive as the mentor's poor judgement and unreliability, which makes us feel extremely uncomfortable. This discomfort comes from cognitive dissonance having been created. If we want to hold on to our belief that the mentor is a wise and reliable person, then it means rejecting the view of someone whose views we respect and value. The other alternative is to hold on to our perception of our colleague as someone whose views we value and respect, and thereby no longer seeing the mentor as someone to be trusted. And so, in order to resolve the contradiction, one set of beliefs has to be abandoned.

This approach draws on the insights that psychology can bring to our understanding of how individuals interact with each other, and we can use this understanding to good effect by creating dissonance in order to throw the attitude or belief we are trying to address into sharp relief. Once it is made obvious to a person that they are holding or expressing two contradictory attitudes or beliefs, then a situation is created where the discomfort caused can become a catalyst for moving forward in his or her thinking. While potentially very effective, it is not an easy technique to adopt and requires careful planning and a subtle approach. It is an advanced tool, rather than a beginner's one.

6.2 Elegant challenging

This technique can be used in similar circumstances to the ones described above, in that it helps to address entrenched attitudes and behaviours by the use of a subtle approach rather than direct confrontation. If we draw on our understanding of human behaviour in general we can appreciate that direct confrontation, especially in a public place or where there are witnesses, has the potential to cause embarrassment. This can then lead on to that person blaming us for making them appear foolish – something which is likely to have adverse effects on our chances, or indeed anyone else's, of addressing the issue in the future. Indeed, it can be the case that the attitudes become even more entrenched in the face of a perceived 'assault' on their views – as in responses such as: 'I've got a right to my own views', and 'Who do you think you are to tell me I can't think or act as I see fit?' While direct confrontation runs the risk of being ineffective in promoting change (for example, in situations where someone consistently uses racist language), so too can ignoring the matter. This is where 'elegant challenging' comes into its own, in that it helps us to raise issues in a way that is perceived as constructive and helpful, rather than as a personal attack.

So, for example, let us imagine a meeting where someone repeatedly refers to migrant workers as 'scroungers and troublemakers'. You are not comfortable with this and can see that other colleagues find her attitude discriminatory. Which of the following options do you think might be more effective in challenging her?

1. Stop her in her tracks during the meeting, tell her you think she is misinformed and that you will not listen any longer to her racist ranting.
2. Find an opportunity as soon as possible after the meeting to engage her in conversation about the issue – perhaps alert her to a well-chosen article or informative website where myths and preconceptions about immigrants are aired.

The second option is more typical of the 'elegant' approach, as it encourages the person concerned to be open to persuasion because you are being reasonable and considerate of her feelings and learning needs, which sets the stage for her to be reasonable in return. Again, this is an approach which requires skill and forethought if it is to work, but isn't that what reflective practice is all about?

Practice focus 4.2

Ffion had been working at the family support centre for over a year and, for the most part, really enjoyed her work. There was just one aspect that worried her. On several occasions she had witnessed one of the volunteers expressing homophobic views quite openly. She didn't want the anti-discriminatory values that underpinned the centre's work to be compromised by this attitude, but felt uncomfortable about raising this issue with the volunteer.

During her next supervision session with her manager, Ffion was encouraged to reflect on her understanding of how learning takes place. This reminded her that a confrontational approach often results in the person who is being criticized becoming defensive to the point where their views become even more entrenched. She had recently read about 'elegant challenging' and decided that, instead of a confrontational approach, she would try being more subtle in helping the volunteer to appreciate how unfair she was being. Over the next few weeks Ffion left articles about anti-discriminatory practice in the staff-room and introduced the topic of homophobia as a case study at one of the regular study sessions that she facilitated at the centre. As she had hoped, there was a lot of discussion within the group, and she noticed that the volunteer in question didn't say much but listened a lot. Ffion had hoped that this more subtle or 'elegant' approach would encourage the volunteer to question her own views and become open to new learning, and it seemed to be working.

6.3 Force-field analysis

This technique has been around for a long time, dating back to Lewin's work in the 1940s. Although not its only application, it can be a very effective way of reflecting-in-action. It involves identifying two sets of factors:

> ■ **Driving forces** – that is, any factor which makes change more likely; and
> ■ **Restraining forces** – those factors that make change less likely to occur.

For example, in a situation where a young boy is refusing to attend school, we might negotiate that he returns to school for two days a week for a specified period. In this instance, the fact that he wants his parents to be proud of him might act as a driving force for change, while peer pressure not to attend school is likely to act as a restraining force in the negotiated change process. Force-field analysis can easily be represented in diagrammatic form, with arrows highlighting whether a particular factor is promoting or inhibiting change. As such, it can help to make the justification for change explicit and facilitate an ethos of partnership in which the commitment for change is more likely to be shared.

In terms of problem solving, force-field analysis will not provide the answer but, as a reflective tool, it will help to 'unpack' the problem by providing a framework for exploring the processes involved. It can be used at an individual or group level and is a good way for practice teachers and mentors to assess a learner's understanding of individual and organizational change processes.

7 Reflection-on-action: question-based frameworks

7.1 What? So what? Now what?

Reflection-on-action involves thinking back over what has happened, and our part in it. However, it is more than just a matter of recalling, as it involves *analysis* of the recollection. As Atkins explains:

> To analyse something, whether an object, a set of ideas or a situation, is to undertake a detailed examination of the structure or constituent parts or elements and ask questions about them, in order to more fully understand their nature and how the parts relate to and influence each other. The term 'critical' introduces a further dimension to analysis, in that judgements are made about the strengths and weaknesses of the different parts as well as of the whole.
>
> (2004, p. 36)

Some find it easier than others to reflect on practice after the event or to add that critical 'edge' to their thinking. Having a framework of questions, or prompts, can therefore be useful aids. The following examples are just three of those that we have come across. One may suit you more than another, or perform better for one purpose than another. If they do not work for you, but inspire you to devise your own, then all to the good. What matters is that we engage in the processes necessary to stop us from 'Bypassing Our Brain' and falling into uncritical and unthinking work practices.

Borton (1970) proposes that practitioners ask themselves the following three questions when engaging in reflection about their work:

> ■ **What?** This requires us to formulate a definition of what has happened or is at issue.
> ■ **So what?** This invites reflection and analysis of that event or issue.
> ■ **Now what?** A stimulus to formulate an action plan, or perhaps outline a learning need.

Those new to the process of reflection may find that they need more in the way of guidance, but a set of questions such as this is easy to remember, and provides at least a starting point. It does require some familiarity with critical thinking skills, without which the second stage cannot happen, but sub-questions can be added to facilitate our own critical reflection. Rolfe, Freshwater and Jasper have built on Borton's three questions in this way in order to help move people on from a descriptive level of reflection to one which incorporates theory and knowledge building and what they refer to as 'action-oriented reflection' (2001, p. 35).

7.2 *Preparing for supervision*

In discussing learning through reflective practice, Bates suggests that prepared case studies be brought to supervision or training sessions, so that an element of analytical thought about why the work was done and what had been learned from it has already taken place. Supervisors and trainers can then build on that analysis, by introducing a critical element, such as is evident in his sample of questions:

> - Did our department/section/organisation act appropriately?
> - Was the response too heavy-handed?
> - Did we do the right thing by the way we acted?
> - How should we have acted in this case to provide a better service?
>
> (2004, p. 26)

This particular set of questions may relate to a specific set of circumstances, but it can serve as an example of how a set of critically reflective questions can be fashioned to suit any situation that is under review. It also reiterates our earlier point that we do not have to rely on 'experts' to provide reflective tools – with a little imagination, we can devise them ourselves.

7.3 *'Prompts'*

While question-based frameworks can be an aid to ordering our thoughts when reflecting on action, these do not necessarily need to be complex or even predefined. For some people a word or phrase can provide enough of a prompt to get those thought processes into gear. For many, the appeal of this is that it is easy to carry those prompts around in our head, and for them to be recalled without too much effort when time is at a premium. In his discussion of learning styles and motivation, Honey suggests getting into a habit of highlighting learning points by using the 'L' word as a prompt:

> In conversations get into the habit of using the 'L' word. 'Something I learned the other day was . . .' 'What I learned from that was . . .' Make it a rule that whenever you indulge in anecdotes and 'war stories' you will explicitly include the lessons you learned.

(2003, p. 24)

This might well work for you, but there are other prompts we have come across, such as:

- **Good/Bad**. What went well today/this week? What didn't?
- **Erase/Rewind**. If I could have the time back, would I have done things differently?
- **Why did I do that?** Can I identify what informed my practice in this instance?
- **Spot check**. Do I feel in control of my workload? Could I explain my aims and objectives in my fields of responsibility if called on to do so now?
- **Humble pie**. Have I been challenged today/this week and learned a lesson from it?
- **Making a difference**. What part did I play in promoting change today/this week? Was it positive or negative change? At what level?

What these words and phrases have in common is that it is relatively easy for them to be recalled, and for the reflection-on-action that they prompt to become a habit – part of the structure of our working day or week and, indeed, an integral part of our workload rather than an add-on to it.

8 Reflection-on-action: emancipatory approaches

8.1 The CIA framework

In all aspects of the helping professions, the potential for workers to feel under pressure is high – it goes with the territory, and it is not uncommon for workers to feel as if there is nothing they can do about the pressures they face. The CIA framework is a tool that can help to prevent that pressure over-spilling into harmful stress. By introducing a sense of realism about what can and cannot be addressed by any one individual, it is an extremely useful exercise for helping to put things into perspective and re-establishing a sense of control when a feeling of powerlessness threatens to overwhelm and demoralize. The CIA framework highlights *Control, Influence* and *Acceptance* as reminders that, whatever we are involved in, there will be things that we can control, things that we cannot control, but which we can influence, and also things that we can neither control nor influence, and so have to accept. Whether we apply this framework to our personal situations or use it when working with others, it can be useful in a number of ways, including:

- **highlighting** what is within someone's control in order to help to challenge negativity and denial about the potential to move forward or address something they do not want to face;
- **focusing** efforts where they are more likely to be effective, thereby countering the risk of setting someone up to fail if he or she is being expected to address something over which they have no control;
- **encouraging** creative thinking about how a situation can be influenced; and
- **concentrating** resources and energy on facilitating acceptance when there is no alternative.

It can therefore be of great help in helping others to see some sort of way forward when the pressures mean they have lost their way or their confidence. In bringing power issues to the fore it helps us to see the bigger picture and our place within it. And, by providing a challenge to self-disempowerment, the CIA framework can be as useful an aid to reflection about self-care as it is to work with disempowered service users.

Voice of experience 4.2

I've been working so hard to help Rita find somewhere to live. She has a learning disability, but everyone agrees that she would manage OK on her own with just a bit of help. But, wherever we've tried, the answer is always the same: 'Sorry, we can't help.' Rita became so demoralized that she wanted to abandon the idea, but I felt bad about that. Then I found out something that made a difference to how we were approaching things – this wasn't about

Rita's learning disability, but about the acute shortage of single-person accommodation in our area. As individuals, we couldn't control that, so we had to accept that this might have to be a long-term goal instead of the main focus of our work together. Now that we have begun to focus instead on how Rita can make her voice heard as a member of her community we have both felt re-energized. I've been putting all my efforts into something that I can't change, but now the role I can play seems to be much clearer.

Drew, an advocate

8.2 *The drawbridge exercise*

This is another technique that helps to focus thinking on the power relations that operate in the social environment in which members of the helping professions operate. It takes the form of an exercise described in Doel and Shardlow (2005) and adapted from Katz (1978). Its purpose is to bring home the existence of differing perspectives and raise the profile of this in terms of respecting diversity and challenging discrimination. This particular exercise involves reading an account of a situation in which someone trying to escape the consequences of her actions ends up being killed, and then exploring which of the six characters in the story should be held responsible for her death. Doel and Shardlow's commentary on the exercise highlights how the apportioning of blame will be influenced by the conceptual framework, or paradigm, from which it is viewed. So, for example, someone looking at the story from a feminist viewpoint might regard the slain woman as the victim of a patriarchal system which sets double standards about fidelity, while, from within a cultural relativist paradigm, the baron who ordered her to be killed was only acting in accordance with what he understood to be 'right and proper' at that time and in that culture.

This exercise can inspire reflection on the significance of differing perspectives, especially in relation to the role of power relations in shaping practice situations. This can then be used to inform future action without reinforcing potentially damaging power inequalities.

9 Reflection-on-action: problem-solving approaches

9.1 *Mind mapping*

While this technique can be used as a planning tool, it can also be very effective in terms of providing the basis for the review and evaluation of practice.

In constructing a visual representation of key ideas and issues, a mind map helps to highlight the connections between them and the potential for ways forward where there are problems – hence the use of the term 'map'. It is based on the work of Tony Buzan and the observation that we do not tend to think in a linear fashion, but jump from one issue to another, especially when under pressure. Figure 4.2 provides an example of a mind map and further examples can be found in Buzan and Buzan (2003) but, very briefly, constructing a mind map involves:

■ Taking a sheet of paper and, using it in 'landscape' layout, writing the focus of the map (a project, problem or whatever) in the centre of the page.
■ Drawing thick lines radiating from this central point, each representing a theme relating to it, and each theme being written in capital letters along the thick line.
■ Drawing thin lines radiating from the top of each thick line, representing sub-themes – these should be spelled out in lower case letters along the length of each thin line.

What results then represents the 'big picture' in diagrammatic form, with the format being conducive to identifying connections between the various strands emanating from the core concept. As a technique it can take some getting used to but, because of its versatility, we would urge you to at least give it a try. The process of constructing the mind map is, in itself, useful for developing thinking skills in general but, more specifically, the technique has the potential to:

■ Get, or recover, a sense of control when overwork or other factors have resulted in our thinking becoming 'fuzzy'.
■ Facilitate creative thinking by making it easier to see the relationship between different aspects of a situation, moving from one to another without losing sight of the overall picture.
■ Highlight an issue (or issues) as particularly crucial or problematic in a situation. For example, the appearance of a particular issue in several places on the map should highlight it as a significant one – something which may not have come to light without the overview that a mind map provides.

Practice focus 4.3

As Ian's supervisor, Karen was aware that one of the cases he had been working on recently had become an increasingly complex one. She had allocated this case to him because, as a final-year student, she felt he needed experience in managing complexity. She knew from her own experience that, with complex pieces of work, it can be difficult to maintain an overview unless the time is made to reflect on what has been happening. And so, at their next supervision session, she introduced Ian to mind mapping, a tool that she had found invaluable in this respect. Together they mapped out what his aims had been and whether progress had been made in any of those areas.

What resulted was a diagrammatic representation of what had been happening since they last met. Karen used this as a basis for exploring problem-solving tactics with Ian, not only in terms of what he was planning to do, but also for evaluating what he had already done. She was heartened to see that, before long, Ian himself was beginning to draw links between what had previously seemed to him to be unconnected issues and to discuss the consequences of his chosen strategies. Ian commented that the process had helped him to see that dealing with issues in isolation was not a good idea, because people don't live their lives like that. Without her suggesting it, Ian came to the next session with all of his casework mapped out in this way and the level of critical reflection rose significantly – a rewarding development for both of them.

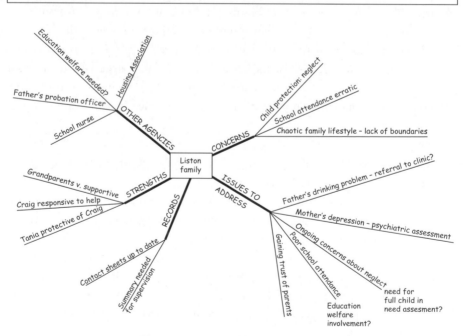

Figure 4.2 Sample of a mind map

9.2 *Process recording*

This technique requires us to focus on what we referred to earlier as the 'space between people' – that is, the processes that are taking place when people interact, such as negotiation, communication, marginalization, avoidance behaviour, reinforcing and so on. When we are busy, we can get so caught up in getting things done that we can lose sight of the significance of these processes. But, while they tend to operate unseen, they are a crucial part of social interaction. Effective practice involves tuning into the existence and significance of these processes at the time of our involvement (reflection-in-action), but also after the event when reviewing and evaluating the work (reflection-on-action). Writing a process recording is something we can do ourselves to help us to focus on the implications of our actions and evaluate the effectiveness of our problem solving, but is also something that those involved in mentoring and assessing can ask of their students and learners.

Rather than just presenting a case study, it involves specifically identifying the processes that have occurred in a situation chosen for review and analysis. A descriptive account might look something like this:

> I met John and his mother at the hospital. He was being interviewed by a police officer while being admitted as a patient because of an injury to his neck. I tried to speak to John, but his mother insisted on speaking on his behalf. He was distressed, but I was unable to speak to a nurse about his condition. I expected the police officer to contact me later but he didn't.

A more process-oriented recording would look more like this:

> For the purposes of information gathering and relationship building I met John and his mother at the hospital. It was clear from what the police officer was saying and from his body language that he was treating him as a suspected criminal and was prioritizing his own duties in this respect over John's physical and emotional needs. I was trying to be an advocate, but his mother was preventing me from doing so by constantly speaking on his behalf, although I am not sure whether she thought she was protecting him or denying him help. He was avoiding eye contact with everyone and exhibiting

> signs of anxiety, such as picking at the bed cover and fiddling with
> his watch and jewellery. The staff there seemed to be embarrassed
> by his mother's emotional outbursts and busied themselves with
> other matters so that they could avoid any potential conflict. As no-
> one from the police service got in touch, I felt that they were
> devaluing my expertise.

Process recording can be an extremely effective tool for 'surfacing' what we often miss and for assessment purposes when we need to know whether a learner has picked up on processes as well as facts.

9.3 Differing perspectives

Doel and Shardlow (2005) describe an activity which they refer to as 'Hold the front page'. It too requires us to make a written record of something we are reflecting on after the event. It is proposed as a tool for learners but, as reflective practitioners are engaged in lifelong learning, it provides an interesting and creative focus for anyone reflecting on action, particularly in terms of diversity. In this activity, we are asked to consider a short case scenario involving a family or group of people. The particular scenario can be followed if you have access to Doel and Shardlow's work but, if not, you can construct your own. The reflection-on-action component of the exercise is to imagine that there is a newspaper devoted to the group or family in our case study. The task is to construct a front page for the newspaper, which will consist of a headline which spells out the main issue (forcing us to think, for example, who in that group has the power to define it) and columns from the various family or group members (who might have competing perspectives on the 'main issue'). Finally, there is the opportunity for 'editorial comment'.

This can be quite an interesting and useful exercise that generates a lot of valuable insights about the significance of difference.

CONCLUSION

This chapter has presented a broad range of tools, techniques or strategies that can be helpful for all three aspects of reflection: reflection-for-action, reflection-in-action and reflection-on-action. Not all of the tools will appeal to all readers or fit with all situations, but we hope we have presented enough techniques and strategies that at least some will be of benefit. Also, as we indicated earlier, we hope that being introduced to the tools outlined here will motivate you to think about developing your own tools – finding structured ways of making sense of the specific practice demands of your work setting and role. This is not something that has to be done alone – many people find that working with others in this way can be a very stimulating and rewarding experience.

Critically reflective practice is about moving away from uncritical, routinized or standardized forms of practice towards more informed, imaginative and value-driven approaches. Tools and techniques can be very helpful in making this move if they are used carefully and skilfully. This chapter will not make that move for us, but it should none the less provide an important basis for taking these matters forward.

Chapter 5

Recording and Assessing Reflection

INTRODUCTION

Many students and award candidates find reflective writing a major struggle and often produce highly descriptive work that is not of a reflective nature. This section therefore explores what is involved in producing reflective and analytical accounts of practice that provide clear evidence of competence in relation to reflective practice. Before looking at what is involved in the actual recording of reflective practice, we first briefly explore *why* and *when* to write reflective accounts. As with any piece of written work, or indeed any piece of work, *why* we are doing it will inform what we need to do and how we need to do it (Thompson, 2003). Furthermore, the value we accord it will influence how much time we devote to it.

Following these discussions, we go on to highlight some of the main characteristics of a good reflective account, whether it be in the form of a reflective log, learning diary or a portfolio of evidence for an award. The final section focuses more specifically on the assessment of reflective practice and, because it contributes towards making assessment processes more transparent, the discussion and guidelines should be just as useful to those being assessed as they are to those doing the assessing.

WHY WRITE REFLECTIVE ACCOUNTS?

There are many reasons for recording reflection, and you can probably come up with more than the brief selection that we have highlighted as being, in our opinion, particularly relevant.

Continuous professional development

Revisiting, reviewing and evaluating our work opens us up to the possibility of learning from both our mistakes and our successes. Reflective accounts, whether shared with others or written in our own format and for our eyes only, provide an example of what Allen, Bowers and Diekelmann (1989) refer to as 'writing-to-learn'. Regardless of any external requirements or 'push factors', taking the initiative in this way can be a stimulating experience, in that it has the potential to provide new insights and also consolidation of previous learning. Jasper's chapter on journals and diaries in Bulman and Schutz (2004) supports this comment and contains some very useful advice on the structuring of learning journals in particular.

> ## Voice of experience 5.1
>
> I've had quite a few articles published in professional journals over the years. Some people ask me where I find the time, but I've always made time for it. It makes me step back from the coalface for a bit and think about what I'm doing and whether I'm making any impact. It's so easy to get sucked into the minutiae.
>
> *Irene, a ward manager*

Accountability

In any profession there will be issues of accountability to consider, be it to those using, managing, funding or overseeing a service. Having written records that document the reflective processes behind decision making can be invaluable in situations where we are called to account for some reason.

Registration requirements

Increasingly, members of the helping professions are being required to make an ongoing case for being considered fit to practise. Reflective accounts can provide evidence to support that case.

Professional credibility

Opening up our practice to the scrutiny of others invites challenge and fosters the growth that can develop from constructive criticism. It can also help to challenge inaccurate stereotypes or assumptions and contribute to making the overall perception of a profession a positive one.

Assessment purposes

Where there is a need to prove competence, especially in terms of being able to practise independently, reflective accounts provide crucial forms of evidence. Especially where portfolios are concerned, the assessment process itself will usually come under scrutiny from an external examiner or assessor whose role it is to help ensure that the process is fair and consistent across a profession. Because an assessor can be called to account for the decisions he or she makes, there has to be demonstrable written evidence in a portfolio to support any assessment of competence that he or she makes.

Practice focus 5.1

It was Greta's first week in her new job after qualifying and she was thinking about how she would fit all of her new responsibilities into a working week. While she was a student she had been required to keep a learning diary so that she could provide evidence that she was practising in a reflective way but, as her workload was expected to increase over the next few weeks, she was glad that she no longer had to make time for it. However, it didn't take long for her to realize how crucial to her learning that process had been and that taking the time to reflect on what had gone and plan for what was to come was vital to her continuing development within the post and the profession. By the third week she had resumed her diary and, each Friday afternoon, she turned off her phone, asked her colleagues not to disturb her and spent the final half-hour of the day reminding herself of what she had learned and had left to learn. Whenever she felt under pressure to use that time for other matters she reminded herself of how unconfident and directionless she had felt in those first few weeks when she had just 'gone with the flow'.

WHEN TO WRITE REFLECTIVE ACCOUNTS

It is not for us, as authors, to be prescriptive about the best time for recording reflection. As we have already seen, reflective practice is not about having arbitrary rules, but about managing our time and commitment to best effect in our own unique circumstances. What follows are just a few points to consider.

Managing time and energy

It may seem obvious to say that the best time is the time that works best for the individual concerned, but it really is a matter of writing when we feel best equipped to do it well – and that will vary from person to person. So, for example, for some people a task requiring clear thinking and concentration is best undertaken before a working day begins, while for others it may become easier to concentrate when other priorities have been dealt with, or during time away from the workplace.

A workable schedule

Again, this is a matter of what works best for each individual, but we would suggest that 'as soon as possible' is a good maxim to adopt. It may be difficult to find the time and energy to make entries in a reflective diary or other such record on a daily basis, although some people find that working in 'bite-size chunks' does work for them. For others, a weekly or monthly programme might work better and some find that a regular and significant event, such as a mentoring or supervision session, serves to focus them on reflection. What matters most is that the process of reflection is regular and consistent, so that it becomes a work habit rather than a one-off or occasional exercise.

Investing the time

Where there are competing demands on time, it is inevitable that some tasks will lose out to others that are given priority over them. The amount of time we invest in recording reflection will therefore be affected by the value we attach to it. A cost-benefit analysis would help to establish whether it is an effective use of time, but we hope by now that we have already convinced you that investing time in the short term will prove beneficial in the longer term. In terms of investment of time, an important factor to consider is how the task is conceptualized. Where finding the time, or the writing process itself, are considered to be chores, then they are more likely to be deferred to other perceived priorities but, if a journal or account is perceived as an aid to practice, rather than a hindrance – in effect, the 'companion' that Ghaye and Lillyman (2006) refer to – then it will be seen as a good investment of time. The reconceptualizing of writing projects as a productive use of time is explored in some depth by Rolfe, Freshwater and Jasper (2001), and we recommend having a look at their ideas – especially if committing time to reflection is a problem.

EXPECTATIONS OF REFLECTIVE ACCOUNTS

In this section we explore what it is that constitutes a good reflective account. The following list of features is not a comprehensive one and we would urge you, as always, to read what other commentators on the subject have to say. These particular points have been chosen because they are among those most often commented on by assessors as lacking in work submitted as evidence of competence. As an aid to understanding, for each of the points discussed, two versions of an account of practice are given. In the first of these (Account A) the particular feature will be lacking, but will be more evident in the second version (Account B).

There is an expectation that a reflective account will have each of the following elements.

An analytical content

Analysis differs from description in that it adds an extra dimension. Descriptive accounts merely give a straightforward account – they tell us about what happened, what a person did or said. But analytical accounts do something extra with that information – they ask questions of it, such as:

- Why was that done?
- What might have happened had the timing been different?
- Was it inevitable that it would end in that way?
- Could things have been done differently? With what effect?

An analytical account will not just mention facts, perceptions and events, but go on to draw links between them, consider alternatives approaches and consequences, explore the beliefs and ideologies that underpin them and so on. You may find it useful to think in terms of the difference in focus between a television drama and a documentary. A drama recounts the story it is concerned with. A documentary, by contrast, goes a step further by not only recounting the story (in summary form at least), but also providing a commentary on it, the significance of certain issues, the recurrence of themes, the interconnections across different elements – in other words, an analysis. Reflective accounts, then, should be more like documentaries than dramas.

Cottrell also offers important comment:

> Analytical writing is writing that looks at the evidence in a detailed and critical way. In particular, it weighs up the relative strengths and weaknesses of the evidence ... so that it is clear how the writer has arrived at judgements and conclusions.
>
> (2005, p. 168)

The following short paragraph is an example of a descriptive account of a practice situation.

> **Account A**
> Last Tuesday I visited Christa because she had rung the office to say that she had been made homeless. The duty officer had told her I would do the visit that same day because it was an emergency, but I was too busy, and so I arranged to go a few days later. When I got there she was sitting outside her flat in a very distressed state and so I took her to a café and bought her a cup of tea to calm her down while I made an appointment for her at the housing department. When I left to go Christa got angry with me because I hadn't sorted out her housing problem. I left her there and went back to the office.

After reading this account we know something of what happened last Tuesday, but nothing about, for example, why this worker did what they did, whether other options had been considered, or what they saw their role as being. The following account has more of an analytical edge to it.

Account B
Last Tuesday the duty officer asked me to visit Christa because she said she had been made homeless. I questioned whether we had enough information to judge whether this was an emergency or not and, on further analysis of the facts available, deferred the visit until I had more time to devote to it and she was better able to think clearly about her future plans now that she had been give notice to leave the flat within the next few weeks. I tried to persuade her to contact the housing department herself because I considered her competent to do so and it would reinforce the assertiveness skills we had been working on, but decided that my own measured approach and good working relationship with the housing department might be more effective in this particular case. Christa was angry with me, because she had expected the problem to be resolved there and then and, while I could understand how frustration and uncertainty had contributed to this heightened state of emotion, I made it clear that it was unhelpful behaviour on her part. We arranged to meet again soon and I returned to the office to consider whether I had played a part in her outburst by not making it clear from the outset that I had no power or even responsibility to allocate housing.

We now have much more of an insight into the situation and the worker's part in that than the first version gave us. It shows us, for example, that this worker is aware of the impact of his or her actions or inactions and that there was a commitment to empowerment and partnership underpinning practice. While Account B is not perfect, as no account will be beyond improvement, it is never the less a significant improvement on A.

Practice focus 5.2

Jonah had been asked to write a reflective account of some recent work he had undertaken in practice, so that he could discuss it with his fellow students on a study day. He had spent a long time on it and so was disappointed when, after asking a colleague to have a look at it, the response was that it needed, in his opinion, to have more depth. When Jonah responded by saying that he had tried to make it as detailed as possible and couldn't see what else he could do, his colleague expanded on his earlier comment by saying that depth and detail were not the same thing and suggested that he think about the purpose of the exercise before doing any revision of his report.

When he did so, he realized that his account, while interesting in itself, would not give his fellow students or his tutor any insight into why he did the work or whether he learned anything as a consequence. When he had reworked his account, the descriptive detail was minimal but the discussion element had increased dramatically. Jonah was surprised to see that the finished account was actually shorter than the original, but was confident that the quality was better. While initially disappointed by the response, he realized that his colleague had done him a favour by criticizing his work in this constructive way.

A critical edge

This is about not taking things for granted. As we noted in Chapter 1, a critical approach is a questioning one, one that 'unpacks' assertions, rather than taking them on board without further thought. For example, there is a 'common sense' view that the loss of a child brings parents closer together. However, Riches and Dawson (2000) present evidence to show that the separation rate is higher, rather than lower, amongst grieving parents. Critical writing shows an awareness of competing perspectives and an understanding that there is rarely a definitive 'right' approach or perspective. At this point, it is worth re-emphasizing Christenson's (2001) argument (quoted in Chapter 2) that a society that wishes to develop creativity also needs to encourage criticism. This is because, if we cannot question our approach and the assumptions on which it is based, we will not realize that there are alternative, possibly better, approaches that we could adopt.

Seeing beyond the worldviews that we acquire as a result of our socialization within a particular culture is not always easy (see the discussions about worldviews in Doel and Shardlow, 2005, and Moss, 2005), but we have to look inwards to our own assumptions as well as those of other people if our written accounts are to be truly reflective.

Consider the differences between the following paragraphs:

Account A
There had been a report of a disturbance down at the youth centre. A local resident had got in touch with me and, as I was the caretaker of the youth club, I made it my business to get involved. I expected there to be trouble, so I let the police know about the situation in case it turned into a full-scale riot. By the time I got

down to the centre there was a crowd of teenagers and everyone was shouting and running wild. While waiting for help to arrive I used a loudspeaker to try to tell them that we weren't going to do anything unless they calmed down and stopped fighting. However, after I got shouted down for the third time and saw a fire being lit I decided to leave it to the police to deal with. After all, it was a law and order issue.

The following account of the same episode, written by the youth leader, shows evidence of critical reflection:

Account B

I was called out to help deal with what was happening at the youth centre. It was described to me by the person who rang me as a 'disturbance' although, to be fair, it would have to have been on a colossal scale to have disturbed anyone, given its location on the empty former industrial estate. When I got there I was alarmed to see a fairly large police presence, as I hadn't realized that things were that serious. And when I negotiated with the police that I go into the building with just one officer I realised that they weren't actually as serious as I had been led to believe. Once I had got everyone to quieten down it became clear that some of them had broken in because they had seen flames and that the shouting and confusion were caused by panic and the fear that they would be blamed for the fire because of stereotypes about a 'typical' teenage lack of respect. Once the police officer had liaised with the fire service and taken witness statements to help with investigations into how the fire was started, everyone left. As I locked up I decided to make sure that the bravery of these young people received acknowledgement in some form, as I was concerned, in the light of the current negative representation of teenagers in the media, that their role might be misrepresented in the reporting of this event.

In the second account, there is evidence that this worker's practice incorporates critical reflection, whereas there is no indication in the caretaker's report that he or she had considered anything beyond their own perspective – that is, it was reported as 'fighting' and 'a law and order issue'. As such, Account A is underpinned by a judgemental attitude, while Account B demonstrates an understanding of the dangers of taking events at face value and not adopting a critical, questioning approach.

Evidence of conceptual thinking

When we write, we do so for a purpose and, for many of those purposes, it is enough to write at a purely descriptive level. When we are planning the route for a day out in the car, say, we do not necessarily think in terms of geographical mobility or the social construction of leisure – we just want a reminder of where to leave the motorway. However, there are times when we do need to think about matters at a different level – that of concepts, rather than simply facts. Reflecting this level of thinking in our writing indicates that we are able to step back and see the bigger picture, the context in which we are operating. If we describe something we have done or seen, then others can surmise something about our observational and descriptive skills from that example. However, if we can comment on what our example is an example *of*, then it indicates a more in-depth level of understanding and analysis.

So, for example, a news report might begin with a description of localized flooding and move on to show interviews with people who have had to move out of their now uninhabitable homes. As such, these examples remain descriptive but, if the report moves on to discuss possible causes and implications, then a conceptual level of analysis is introduced. That is, there will be discussion about what this event is an example *of* – inadequate flood planning, population relocation, disenfranchised loss or whatever. Where this level of analysis is present in reflective accounts, it is a good indicator that the person writing it appreciates the need to account for the context, or rather contexts, in which he or she practises.

Consider the following account which is written in a fairly descriptive way:

Account A

As a nurse, I have been required to work to a rota which includes night shifts. I didn't expect this to be a problem as long as I could get the same amount of sleep as I would when working during the day and sleeping at night. However, I think that my practice has

suffered because of it. Last week, for example, I found myself referring to a patient by the wrong name and failed to notice that
another patient had gone missing from the ward. I resolved to get
more sleep but, even though I did so, I still felt tired. In work everything seemed to take twice as long to do, especially as I often had
to call on a colleague to check things out because I recognized that
my concentration wasn't as sharp as it should have been. I asked a
friend who had worked on the night shift for years how I could
adapt. He said that he hadn't had a problem when he was regularly
working nights, but had experienced similar problems since being
required to move between day and night shifts on the new rota.
This conversation made me feel better.

As such, it documents an experience but does not provide any evidence to
suggest that the person writing the account understands what his or her experience is an example of. The way in which Account B is written is not just a
'fancier' way of describing the same situation – it moves the writing on to a
different level which adds something extra. For example, the use of concepts,
such as resource management and sleep deprivation, provides some indication
that this person can locate individual experiences in a wider context and
appreciates conceptual links:

Account B
As a nurse, I have been required to work to a rota which includes
night shifts. I didn't expect this to be a problem as long as my usual
sleep patterns were not disturbed by the irregular work cycle that
had been introduced by the Trust as a new measure. I was aware
that there is a link between irregular shift patterns and sleep deprivation, but didn't think it would affect me too much. However, I
think my practice has suffered as a consequence. Last week, for
example, my recall and observational skills became impaired on a
number of occasions. At the time I assumed that my failure to adapt
was the problem but, after sharing experiences with a friend, I
began to see the bigger picture. Maybe this wasn't about me and
other individuals being poor copers, but about poor human
resource management and insufficient research into the links
between shift patterns and concentration levels. After talking to him
I felt less inadequate and developed a heightened awareness of the
organizational context of my practice.

An appreciation of one's own role in change processes

As we have noted, central to reflective practice is self-awareness. In the helping professions we often use ourselves as a means to promote change. That is, it is something that we do or say, or the way we do or say it that makes a difference. For example, when someone is faced with a serious loss or a frightening change of circumstances, the fact that we validate their experiences as traumatic, thereby giving them 'permission' to have strong emotional reactions, can make a very positive contribution to their being able to cope. But, as Thompson comments, if we use tools we need to understand them:

> In working with people, our own self or personality is often used as a tool, a means by which positive change can be facilitated. This is perhaps the most obvious reason for encouraging self-awareness – using a tool without knowing what it is or how it works can hardly be seen as a wise basis for practice.
>
> (2002, p. 3)

As people working with people, it is inevitable that we will have an impact on the dynamics of any situation and, without recognition of this, any written account of practice will be missing an important dimension in terms of reflective content. As with the previous points, the difference between the following two accounts should help to highlight what is expected in a reflective commentary:

> **Account A**
> When I heard the news that Donald's wife, Sharida, had died I went to see him as soon as I could manage. I had been Sharida's care manager for several years and knew how difficult it had been for both of them as Sharida's chronic condition took its toll on her health. I was aware that the funeral arrangements were being taken care of by a relative, but I was worried about how Donald would cope afterwards. I realized that his role as a full-time carer had impacted on his social network and that he had grown apart from many of his former friends. On my next visit I took along the details

of several clubs and societies which I thought might tempt him to socialize again, but found that he was reluctant to do so. I wondered whether a support group for bereaved carers might help, but he just became upset when I broached the subject. I thought he would have welcomed it.

Account B

When I heard the news that Donald's wife, Sharida, had died I went to see him as soon as I could manage, having made sure that he was ready to receive visitors. I had been Sharida's care manager for several years and knew how difficult it had been for both of them as Sharida's chronic condition took its toll on her health. I was aware that both of them had faced multiple losses, including the cancellation of their long-planned retirement trip to Sharida's home country. Donald seemed to cope quite well with the physical demands of his role as carer but not the emotional ones and so I had always made time to ask about his feelings and to reassure him that they were only to be expected in the situation he was facing. I had come to know Donald as a resilient person and felt sure that he would be able to rekindle old friendships and make new ones once he had given himself time to grieve after Sharida's death, but I felt I still had a role to play in helping him come to terms with his feelings of loss, even though I knew I could not take the pain away. When I evaluated my input into this case I thought about whether I had achieved what I had set out to achieve – and I had. My aim had been to help Donald and Sharida to understand what was going on in their lives and to reassure them that their 'anticipatory grieving' was a well-documented and healthy response (Corr, Nabe and Corr 2006) and not at all 'weird and unnatural', as some people had described it. It became clear from Donald's comments after the funeral that my insight had been a key factor in his coping strategy.

In the first of these accounts the writer seems to perceive him- or herself as simply a 'signpost' to other services. The second, however, demonstrates an awareness of how one's own knowledge, skills and values can constitute very effective tools in themselves.

An awareness and understanding of complexity

The world of the helping professions is full of ambiguities and uncertainties which make it virtually impossible to predict outcomes or prescribe the 'right' answer or approach – not that this stops some people trying to do so! As we have seen, reflective practice is about rising to the challenge of dealing with complexity, rather than trying to find the nearest acceptable match between a problem and an existing, ready-made solution. Experience equips us with evidence that some approaches have worked well in some circumstances and that it might be worth bearing this in mind rather than 're-inventing the wheel' on each occasion. But, it should not obscure the unique complexities within each new situation.

Responding to a problem as if it has just one dimension is an example of 'essentialism', a term which refers to the tendency to explain behaviour in terms of fixed qualities or 'essences'. An example of essentialism would be the assumption that all violent crimes carried out by women are caused by the effects of hormonal imbalances on behaviour. An anti-essentialist response would argue that, while hormonal imbalance might be a factor in some cases, it would not be the only factor in those cases, nor might it even be a factor at all in other cases. In each case of murder there could be any number of possible factors to take into account, such as domestic violence, poverty, mental health problems, jealousy, revenge, pity and so on.

There is an expectation, therefore, that a good reflective account will demonstrate an understanding of the complexity and uncertainty that characterizes work in the helping professions. We can see that the following account is lacking in this respect:

Account A

As part of my course I spent some time shadowing a worker at a refuge for women trying to escape from domestic abuse. As I got to know some of the women better, I noticed that there were similarities in their personality and behaviour. They were all really disorganized and, once they have settled in at the refuge, they didn't seem to want to do anything to help themselves. I was only going to be there for a couple of weeks, so I was keen to be as helpful as I could while I was there, but no-one seemed interested in getting themselves onto the refuge's resettlement programme. Having read

> about 'victim behaviour', I'm pretty sure that this was what was happening here. And, if they lived their lives in this way, they were probably inviting their partners to be abusive. It must be frustrating to live with someone who can't seem to organize themselves or their lives and expects someone else to solve their problems for them. I learned a lot about psychology during those two weeks.

By contrast, this account does not make the same mistake:

> **Account B**
>
> As part of my course I spent some time shadowing a worker at a refuge for women trying to escape from domestic abuse. As I got to know some of the women better, I noticed that there were similarities in their personality and behaviour. They were all really disorganized, but I could see that this was only to be expected, given that they had all probably had to leave home in a hurry. Maybe some of them had planned this well in advance though, and it was only because they had such good organizational skills in the first place that they had managed to get out of the abusive situation relatively safely? I wondered whether I could have been 'organized' in that tiny room at the refuge when I had all those mixed feelings running through my head: Was I really safe here? What would happen now? Would I ever feel safe again? Will I have enough money to live on? I wanted to help, but found that my offers were not welcome. At first I took it personally but, on reflection, realized that it was probably a matter of poor timing. Perhaps some of the women weren't ready to think of moving forward yet, because they were still thinking about what they had lost. I had read about 'victim behaviour' and wondered whether this had any bearing on the situations I was witnessing. Maybe it was a factor in some cases, but I couldn't accept that it was universal or that a particular way of behaving could cause or legitimize abuse. I wondered whether the experience of domestic violence would have robbed me of my confidence and skills too. I learned a lot about domestic violence in those two weeks and a lot about myself. I would not allow myself to be seduced by simplistic reasoning – people's problems are never simple because people are complex and they live multifaceted lives.

We can see that Account A has been written in a very dogmatic way, with her perspective being presented as the 'true' one and underpinned by the assumption that a complex phenomenon (in this case domestic violence) can be explained by just one factor (the way in which some women behave). The second account demonstrates a far more sophisticated understanding of the complexities of human life.

It is to be hoped that our comments here, combined with the contrasting examples given, will paint a helpful picture of what is needed to produce genuinely reflective writing that is not simply descriptive. We now turn to the issue of assessing reflective accounts. This discussion should cast some additional light on writing reflective accounts. We therefore recommend that you read the next section, even if you are not involved as an assessor of reflective accounts.

ASSESSING REFLECTIVE ACCOUNTS

The role of an assessor or examiner is to ensure that an account which claims to, or is required to, demonstrate evidence of reflective practice actually does so. It should come as no surprise, then, that much of what follows in this section is informed by the discussion in the previous one. There would be little point in revisiting that material here other than to reiterate the point that such evidence, when presented in reflective accounts, needs to be explicit rather than implicit if an assessor or examiner is to be able to use it as an indicator of success. If part of what constitutes reflective practice is being clear about what we are trying to achieve and whether we have achieved it, then an account which requires the assessor to work out the implications for him- or herself is unlikely to be convincing evidence.

We would hope that the expectations outlined in the previous section will provide a good foundation from which to develop in terms of assessing reflective practice. What follows are some further thoughts on what might indicate that a person's practice has the 'mindful' basis expected of a reflective practitioner.

When examining a portfolio or other form of reflective writing, then, we need to ask whether there is evidence of the following.

An awareness of interactive processes

Descriptive work tends to focus on people in a reported scenario, but failure to acknowledge what happens, or fails to happen, in 'the space between people' is a significant omission. We need to be seeing evidence of a heightened sensitivity to processes, as this is where much of our work in the helping professions operates. For example, a descriptive account might record that, during a heated exchange of views, someone got up and left the room. It tells us facts but does not reflect an understanding of the processes that might have been occurring, such as the playing out of a power relationship or the avoidance of conflict.

Creativity

There needs to be evidence that each presenting problem is responded to in a way that addresses the uniqueness of that problem, rather than by an uncritical 'going through the motions'. Where there was no existing appropriate response, has one been created?

Learning and development

Given that reflective practice is about the integration of theory and practice, there needs to be evidence not only that learning has taken place, but of how it has been integrated into practice – in effect, the consequence of the learning has to be evident.

An up-to-date knowledge base

Sometimes candidates present evidence of the knowledge base that has informed their practice, but it is clear that it has not been critically reviewed for some time. Theoretical paradigms that have been influential for many years will have been challenged by other theorists who have a different perspective. Where competing perspectives are not explored, and outdated or even discredited theories are used as supporting evidence, it does little to convince an assessor that a practitioner has his or her 'finger on the pulse' of developments in their particular field and is working 'safely' within their particular codes of practice.

Voice of experience 5.2

I've been assessing portfolios for a few years now, but I still find it difficult when I have to return one because it doesn't convince me that that this person practises reflectively. To counterbalance that, I have to remember that I owe it to the vulnerable members of our society to help ensure that a sound knowledge and value base informs the practice of those who work with them.

Tony, a team manager and practice teacher

An explicit value base

As we noted in Chapter 3, values have such an influence on actions and attitudes that it would be worrying if the values that underpin practice were not given a high profile in something submitted as evidence of reflective practice. We are all influenced by values, even though we may not be aware of it, as, by their very definition, values are what we hold dear. We live our lives according to what we value, and this applies to our professional lives too – what we think of as important will have an influence on what we do. In a reflective account, these influences and the learning that results from the process of 'surfacing', have to be explicit if we are to convince anyone that we are practising in a 'mindful' way. As Thompson comments:

> a worker may not be explicitly aware that he or she subscribes to a particular value (the importance of human dignity, for example) but none the less act fully in accordance with this (implicitly held) value. However, it can be argued that the more conscious we are of our own values, the more we are able to ensure that our actions are consistent with them.
>
> (2005, p. 109)

Selectivity

A good reflective account does not necessarily have to be a long one. It is often the case that the better ones are also the shorter ones, because they are not 'padded out' with irrelevant material that is superfluous and adds nothing in the way of evidence of reflective practice. Indeed, the inclusion of superfluous material can even be a negative indicator – that is, it can be considered as evidence that the person presenting the material does not really understand what it is that he or she is trying to achieve. For example, we have seen directions to a training event and the fire regulations at a course venue being included in a portfolio of evidence! The only positive indicator we could see on that occasion was that this person could put paper into a binder competently, while it seriously undermined our assessment of that person as a reflective practitioner who understood aims, objectives and strategies.

An awareness of comparative practice

Doel and Shardlow (2005) make the point that a lot can be learned about practice and one's role by considering how it is, or has been, conceptualized in different places and in different eras. For example, one might consider whether the present understanding of a nursing, social work or teaching role bears any similarity to how those roles were conceptualized in, say, the 1950s, or how the roles have developed in other parts of the world. Of course, the absence of such a perspective is only a problem if it had been specified particularly as a required area of competence but, if such an inquisitive element were to be included, it would add useful support to a claim to reflective practice.

Motivation

A reflective practitioner will be committed to making his or her practice as informed as possible. One would therefore expect a good reflective account to show evidence not only of an awareness of the importance of directives and updates circulated to them by their employers, but also of being proactive in keeping up to date with developments in his or her particular area of expertise. Reference to independently sought literature, research reports, media comments, journal articles and so on would suggest that this person is an independent thinker and well motivated to learn although, of course, the reference alone and without any analysis would not be convincing.

Recognizing competing perspectives

This ties in closely with the point about complexity discussed earlier. There will always be a variety of perspectives on any situation, and it would be arrogant for anyone to propose that their take was the 'right' one. A piece of writing that does not reflect differing perspectives or promotes a particular theoretical approach without recognition of any challenges to it is unlikely to count as evidence of reflective writing, because it underplays the complexity of work in the helping professions and indicates an uncritical approach. With reference to presenting reasoned arguments, Cottrell highlights the importance of 'signposting' critical awareness:

> A strong argument will usually critically evaluate alternative perspectives or points of view. By doing so, authors show readers that they have considered other possibilities and not simply presented the first argument that entered their heads. This approach usually strengthens an argument as it suggests that the author has researched the subject or has considered all angles.
>
> (2005, p. 175)

She suggests the word 'alternatively' or the phrase 'it might be argued that' as signalling a recognition of competing perspectives, and to these we would add 'on the other hand' and 'however' as indicators that the writing is taking a critical turn. In the helping professions very little is straightforward and dilemmas are common. We would therefore expect any critically reflective account of practice to reflect a diversity of perspectives and approaches.

And finally, we need to make specific mention of assessment criteria. These provide the standards against which competence is judged and ought therefore to be helpful frameworks for both candidates and assessors/examiners. However, in our experience, it is often the case that many candidates, particularly when submitting portfolios, present what they want to present rather than what they are *asked* to present, and that any match between evidence and criteria seems to be coincidental. Some would argue that the best portfolios are the ones that make the links between criteria and evidence explicit, so that the assessor does not have to make those links for him- or herself. We would suggest, however, that anything else is indicative of a lack of planning or understanding of the task in hand – 'winging it' by presenting a poorly constructed portfolio of evidence hardly gives a positive message of reflective practice to an assessor!

It can help in this respect for someone compiling a portfolio to take a step back and imagine that they are the assessor or examiner reading it, rather than the candidate writing or compiling it. This process acts as a cross-check against criteria because it begs the question: 'If an assessor needs to find this or that evidence, will they be able to find it amongst the detail and, indeed, is it there at all?' Those who have had experience of learning on programmes that use self- or peer assessment may feel more comfortable with this way of working, precisely because it forces them to look at the assessor/examiner perspective.

Practice focus 5.3

Sal and Ali had both been participants on a reflective practice workshop. They had attended because they both carried a responsibility, as part of their jobs, for promoting and assessing reflective practice in others. By talking to each other about their experiences, they realized that both of them found it difficult to explain to candidates what was meant by making their evidence of reflective practice explicit rather than implicit. They raised this issue with the rest of the group and found one particular response very helpful in this respect. Evan explained that he reminded those he supervised that any portfolio of evidence they presented would probably be read by someone who, unlike him, knew nothing about them and had not been party to any discussions about the work that he or she had been doing. Therefore, they would need things spelling out for them, because nothing could be taken as read or inferred from prior knowledge of people or situations. Both Sal and Ali realized that this was a very useful starting point for helping students to understand why they had to make the evidence explicit and food for thought on how they could do so.

Finally, in terms of assessing reflective writing, we offer a checklist developed by one of the present authors in his role as an external examiner to an educational programme for which evidence of reflective practice was a requirement. It incorporates much of what we have discussed in this chapter, and so we include it here, as both assessors and candidates may find it useful.

Checklist for assessors/examiners
- Does the candidate make clear the basis of the work undertaken – the rationale, policy context and so on?
- Does the candidate show evidence of drawing on a professional knowledge base – not just tokenistically mentioning a theoretical approach, for example, but showing an understanding of why it is appropriate in this instance?

- Does the candidate present *explicit* evidence of the required aspects or levels of competence? Is there evidence to indicate that the candidate has understood that the responsibility for demonstrating evidence lies with him or her?
- Does the candidate show evidence of a value base to their practice? Merely mentioning values-related words is not enough – there needs to be evidence of an understanding of why something is significant, what it would mean if a particular value were not respected, and so on.
- Does the candidate adopt an analytical approach? Is the approach to practice clear, focused and critical?
- Is there evidence of a commitment to continuing development? A reflective practitioner recognizes that the helping professions are a complex and evolving field.

With its focus on assessment of competence, the discussion in this section serves to reinforce the responsibility that rests on the shoulders of those doing the assessing to make sure that the standards expected of a reflective practitioner within a particular profession are maintained. While taking this 'gate-keeping' responsibility seriously, we must not forget that as reflective practice is about growing and developing, there is also a responsibility to promote learning through the assessment process. Doel, Sawdon and Morrison remind us that our approach to assessment has the potential to discourage, as well as encourage learning:

> There is an inherent power differential between assessor and assessed. Learners submit their work to assessment systems which have the power to make judgements, and these judgements can find the learner wanting. Similar imbalances are to be found in practitioners' own work, where they are expected to develop empowering partnerships with service users, clients and patients. How can the assessment arrangements and methods ensure that learners experience the assessment as one which leaves them feeling more rather than less powerful, while respecting the need for external scrutiny of professional practice and, ultimately, the sanction of failure to license for practice? It is important that the programme's teaching on values such as empowerment is reflected in the way those values are assessed. In this way, individuals will be encouraged to learn from the process rather than to approach it defensively.
>
> (2002, p. 48)

CONCLUSION

Producing and assessing reflective accounts can be demanding work, but it can also be very rewarding and productive. Both make an important contribution to maximizing learning and enhancing professional practice. We hope that the guidance and food for thought that we have provided in this chapter will be a valuable aid to your efforts in these areas.

As we have seen, there are no simple formulas to follow, but there are points of guidance that help us navigate our way through the complexities of developing critically reflective practice. In this respect, what is expected in terms of writing about, and assessing, reflective practice mirrors the process of reflective practice more broadly – mindfully working our way through the challenges that befall us in an effort to make a positive difference.

That process will often involve encountering obstacles, but we are then able to focus our critically reflective faculties on addressing those obstacles – and it is to this that we now turn as the subject matter of Chapter 6.

Chapter 6

Barriers to Reflective Practice

INTRODUCTION

Our experience of running training courses on the subject of critically reflective practice has helped us to identify a wide range of actual or potential obstacles to reflective approaches. These range from individual factors, such as attitude and skills, to issues about workplace culture and organizational expectations. In a short chapter such as this, there is not the space for us to mention every problem we have come across, and so we have chosen instead to highlight just a few of those factors and explore why they present significant obstacles; and provide some food for thought on developing strategies to address them

We hope that these discussions inspire you to review your own situation and, if you are struggling with reflective practice, to identify where the problem lies in your particular case. Armed with this insight, you will be better equipped to formulate an action plan that suits both your needs and your timetable.

We have chosen six concerns as representative of the many obstacles, both real and perceived, that can get in the way of a reflective approach to practice. Given that the key premiss underpinning reflective practice is that there are no simple, 'off the peg' answers to complex issues, we cannot give you any definitive solutions to the obstacles you might face – nor would we want to. What we can do is to validate those concerns and provide a starting point for thinking about the strategies you can adopt in your own particular circumstances.

A common theme across the discussions presented in this chapter is the significance of the organizational context and the pressures it brings. It should therefore be borne in mind that many of the suggestions we make here relate to influencing that context – that is, not only shaping our own practice, but also seeking to influence the organization in a positive direction. Given the key role of organizational factors in either helping or hindering reflective practice, there is much to be gained by trying to think of tackling obstacles as a *collective* challenge as well as an individual one, with people pulling together to promote critically reflective approaches wherever possible.

TIME CONSTRAINTS

Perhaps the most commonly heard comment from practitioners attending training courses and workshops on the subject of reflective practice is: 'I'm too busy to take time out for reflection.' While many people feel reasonably comfortable in saying that, what this can amount to is an admission to practising in an unthinking or 'mindless' fashion. Busy schedules call for setting priorities, but for many people taking time out to think about what they are doing and how and why they are doing it is seen as a luxury – rather than as integral to the job of being a professional practitioner. Comments like: 'I'm a practitioner, not an academic' and 'If you've got time to think, then you obviously haven't got enough work to do' convey an understanding of practice and the theory and knowledge that informs it as two distinct and separate spheres. Where they are seen as separate issues, then the potential is high for one to be prioritized over the other, especially if the latter is conceptualized as not being 'real' work. But where they are seen as an integrated whole, then the reflective aspect no longer loses out to the practice aspect, but supports it. And, in informing practice, it can make that practice more focused and more effective, thereby saving time in the long run. It can also mean fewer mistakes, fewer complaints or other dissatisfactions and higher levels of morale and motivation. We have to ask ourselves, therefore, whether this oft-claimed barrier to reflective practice is perceived rather than actual. As we noted in Chapter 1, the busier we are, the more reflective we need to be. The issue of time is therefore a complex one, and we do ourselves (and the people we serve) a significant disservice if we reduce it to simple complaints that we 'don't have enough time'.

Practice focus 6.1

Jenny was the supported housing unit's duty officer on the afternoon that a referral was made by a community nurse who had expressed concern about Mr Roberts' independent living skills. As was the custom and practice, she made arrangements to visit Mr Roberts within the next 24 hours. Unfortunately this meant that she was unable to attend a meeting that had been called some time ago to discuss plans for a multidisciplinary response to crisis situations in the local area. She had been keen to attend but, as she was the only person available to make the visit, she sent her apologies to the meeting's convenor and went to see Mr Roberts.

Once back she was asked by her manager why she had not attended such a crucial meeting. Jenny's response that she had been too busy did not go down well and prompted her to think about whether, in retrospect, there had been any choice in the matter. In order to help clarify her thoughts she took a sheet of paper and wrote down the possible costs and benefits of prioritizing one demand on her time over the other. This task took only 10 minutes of her day, but helped her to realize that missing the meeting was going to prove very costly in terms of her time over the coming weeks, because she would have to make the organization's potential contributions and constraints known to each of the other organizations' representatives, but on an individual basis now and six times over. She also realized that the 24-hour response had not only been unnecessary, as there was no official policy to that effect but also, after revisiting some client feedback about the frustration caused by the lack of a 'seamless assessment process', might even have proved to be counterproductive. What the day's events had brought home to her was that time used to take stock of a situation and to think through her objectives would be time well spent on future occasions.

If, for whatever reason, finding time is proving to be an obstacle, then you might find the following strategies useful.

Incorporating thinking time

Conceptualizing reflection as part of your workload rather than as separate from it should prompt you to incorporate time for reflection (whether it be reflection-for-action or reflection-on-action) into your workload plans. For example, if you are due to attend a meeting from 2 o'clock until 4 o'clock, then you could plan to take three rather than two hours out of your normal schedule, thereby giving yourself the time necessary to plan what you hope to achieve in that meeting and time afterwards to reflect on the implications that have arisen from it. In this way you have *made* the time to do the whole task (physically attending the meeting *and* getting the best from it). Thinking about the meeting and the reflection as two different things may result in one being prioritized over the other if time is short, but seeing them as part and parcel of the same task should help prevent that from happening. It might help, when planning, to picture yourself acting out your diary or work plan. If you can see yourself rushing from room to room, house to house, department to department or appointment to appointment, and then trying to find time to make sense of it all by picking up the pieces later, then you might want to give this strategy some thought.

Spending time to save time

When we are under a lot of pressure it can be tempting to 'get stuck in' so that we can feel a sense of progress but, because working with people and their problems is unpredictable, it is highly unlikely that an unplanned and routine response will 'hit the spot' every time, if ever. If you have ever been in the position of having invested a lot of time in tackling something, only to find that the time has been wasted (perhaps because of a misunderstanding, for example) then you will appreciate how frustrating that can be. If you think that you do not have the time for reflective practice, then you might ask yourself whether you have time to waste, because that is the risk that we run if we rush into acting without thinking about what should inform that action, or fail to analyse it so that we can learn from mistakes and build on successes.

You might find it useful to think back over your own practice and see whether you can remember instances where you:

■ wasted time in circumstances where you could have avoided this by spending time initially in ensuring that what you did was focused and appropriate; or
■ despite being busy, invested some of that precious time in ensuring that the little time you did have was used most effectively.

This exercise, whether carried out alone (the personal reflective space referred to in Chapter 3) or with colleagues (in dyadic or group reflective space) can be very effective in bringing home the point that a reflective approach, while requiring a little extra time to begin with, has the potential to repay that investment many times over.

Taking control of your workload

In situations where work is allocated by a line manager, it can take courage to refuse to take on more work when you are feeling that you do not have the time to deal with what you already have on your plate. Similarly, if there is an 'open door' policy where you work, so that there is no mechanism for regulating the amount of work coming in, it can be difficult to suspend or stem the flow. However, if we do bow to the pressure, and that pressure to 'get things done' means that we do not have time to think about what we are doing, then the potential for things to go wrong is high. If we do not want to run the risk of practising dangerously, then it is important to be assertive about the right to have a manageable workload. The following example highlights the importance of taking responsibility for creating the time to practise reflectively – for ensuring that we do not have to take shortcuts to fit too big a workload into a finite number of hours.

Voice of experience 6.1

I feel like giving in my notice. All I seem to do is deal with emergency situations that only arise because I haven't got time to deal with the underlying issues that contribute to the emergencies in the first place. And that isn't a good situation to be in for me or my clients. I noticed that a colleague was reviewing her work projects by writing action plans for each one and I thought it would help me to do the same. I became even more demoralized when I realized that I had lost sight of my aims and couldn't identify them. I'm going to tell my manager that I won't take on any new work until I can deal appropriately with what I already have on my plate. I won't resign, but I will claim the time I need to be the reflective practitioner that I need and want to be – and that I know I can be.

Fran, a community psychiatric nurse

WANING COMMITMENT

Denying or minimizing the value of reflective practice can prove a difficult barrier to overcome. This is because, where something is not valued, it is unlikely to be seen as useful or a worthwhile investment of time and effort. The lack of commitment can manifest itself at an individual level for some people, but it is also not uncommon for it to pervade the culture of a team or staff group or even of a whole organization. Where colleagues fail to value reflective practice, then those who do take time to plan and evaluate can get singled out as 'thinkers' rather than 'doers', which can then lead to a culture of blame when workloads are high and reflective time is perceived as a luxury. Where a routinized and uncritical response from staff is not only accepted, but actually sanctioned by managers, then this can prove to be a significant barrier to those who see reflection-for, reflection-on and reflection-in-action as crucial to their role as members of the helping professions and therefore as a legitimate use of time, *especially* when workloads are high.

We also have to think about commitment in terms of accountability. Professionalism incorporates accountability at a number of levels (for example, to the client, to the profession and to society), and so an approach that relies on 'common sense' and untested assumptions to address problems runs a very high risk of compromising accountability. How can we account for decisions made and actions taken, or not taken, if we are unable to account for what informed those actions or decisions?

Furthermore, where there is little or no commitment to critical and informed practice, there is often also a degree of complacency about the efficiency and effectiveness of the work being carried out. Routines have their place, but the world of the helping professions is a complex and changing one where the uniqueness of each situation is unlikely to be adequately met by a routine response. Routines tend to be based on long-held assumptions, such as: 'We've always done it this way here – things have gone well this far, so why change things now?' There is an element of arrogance in this type of approach, as it assumes that the 'way it has always been done' *is* as effective as it is made out to be. How can we *know* that in any objective sense, unless it is opened up to the critical analysis that underpins a reflective approach? (See the discussion of open vs. closed knowledge in Chapter 1.)

Strategies for overcoming such barriers will obviously differ according to where the lack of commitment lies, and so the following suggestions reflect this.

Document your learning

Where the lack of commitment is your own, we would once again stress how useful it can be to get into the habit of keeping a reflective log or diary, even if only for a short time. If you devise a system for highlighting key issues, learning points and so on (perhaps by using a highlighter pen, or writing keywords or questions in the margin – see Jasper, 2003, or Rolfe, Freshwater and Jasper 2001, for more ideas about this), then you will find that you can 'surface' (that is, make explicit) the factors that make your work harder or easier, more or less effective and so on. In this way you are likely to become more and more convinced of the benefits of, and become more committed to, adopting a reflective approach.

Show by example

Where there is a lack of commitment to reflective practice, it is often because of a misunderstanding of what it is about and why it is important (see Chapter 1). Where you are committed to it, but colleagues are reluctant to accept that a reflective approach could enhance their practice, a useful strategy is to show them examples of how it enhances your own. Where there is cynicism about the relevance of 'theory' to practice, seeing how it can inform practice in a positive way can help to overcome this. Planting the seed in people's minds in this way can be more effective in terms of overcoming a lack of commitment than quoting the very works that those who 'stick to practice' tend to want to avoid.

Address accountability

We would hope that people come to see the benefits of reflective practice for its own sake – because they want to practise to the best of their abilities and continue to grow professionally. However, even where there is no commitment in that sense, then the need to be accountable for our actions can also consti-tute a 'push factor'. While we would not endorse a 'cover your back' approach to practice, it can nevertheless be useful to challenge a lack of commitment by talking to colleagues about accountability (perhaps putting the subject on the agenda at a team or staff meetings) and letting them know how practising reflectively has contributed to how you feel confident that you would be able to account for your actions, should you ever be in a position where your competence is challenged (see the discussion below about profes-sional registration).

ORGANIZATIONAL CULTURE

We have seen that the negative attitude of some individuals can be a factor in downplaying the importance of reflective practice, and how this can be reinforced by team or organizational cultures that see reflective practice as a threat or a nuisance. However, a lack of commitment, or even active resistance, to it at an organizational level can also be a significant barrier to progress. As Thompson argues:

> In terms of integrating theory and practice, a culture characterised by negativity and helplessness will stand in the way of a positive practice premised on critical reflectivity . . . A negative culture is therefore a serious barrier to integrating theory and practice, as it relies on routine standard responses to problems and situation, rather than reflection, critical analysis or creativity.
>
> (2000, p. 131)

There are a number of reasons why an unsupportive, or sometimes even an 'anti-learning', culture may exist within an organization. These can include:

■ A focus on what has come to be known as 'managerialism' operating at the expense of other interests. The rationalist approach to policy implementation remains an influential one in the helping professions (Baldwin, 2004), and its target-driven philosophy can stifle those who feel that a less directive and more value-driven approach is what is needed.

■ The conceptualization of members of the helping professions as bureaucrats employed to carry out their employers' instructions, rather than as professional problem solvers with decision-making skills and the expertise to work with a degree of autonomy. The following comment by Baldwin offers a helpful perspective:

> One of the tenets of effective organizational learning is that it is there to manage the uncertainties of organizational life and, indeed, to use them as a positive force for change and development. To attempt to manage out uncertainty is to destroy the potential opportunities for dynamic creativity present in managing uncertainty.
>
> (2004, p. 48)

■ A sense of mistrust about change. Fook (2004) highlights the diversity of interests which can exist within organizations and inhibit the development of a learning environment. Referring to the work of Argyris and Schön (1978), she makes the following point:

> They presented as issues of diversity, the need to recognize the politics involved because of a diversity of interests, and how new practical issues may emerge and change during the course of implementation rather than being predictable beforehand. What is a welcome change to some will be a threat to others; what is experienced as empowering for workers may be seen as disempowering for managers.
>
> (Fook, 2004, p. 72)

■ Anti-intellectualism. In addition to workplace culture issues in their own right, there will be factors at the level of whole professions or disciplines, not least an emphasis on the 'practical' at the expense of the underpinning knowledge and values that are needed to make sure that such practice is safe and ethically acceptable.

Practice focus 6.2

Remy had been part of the team for over three years now and was becoming increasingly disappointed at the lack of enthusiasm for his suggestion to have a group discussion about the benefits of reflective practice. Directives about policy change were coming through to the team very regularly and he perceived them as cost-cutting exercises which had the potential to compromise the values that the team was meant to espouse. Few of his colleagues showed any interest, and his manager even told him to forget about 'all that college stuff' and concentrate on tackling the backlog of referrals.

Remy thought long and hard about the lack of interest he was encountering. To some extent he could understand the financial pressures, but struggled to understand why his colleagues were showing no concern about the implications of the new policies for the lives of the people they were supposed to be helping. This got Remy thinking about the culture of his workplace and how it had changed since he first joined the team. At one time there had been a strong sense of injustice which had led people to challenge policy decisions that would have unfavourable consequences for vulnerable people. Lately, though, there was a sense of defeatism and people were enacting the new policies without questioning whether there was a different and better way.

He wondered whether this could help explain the lack of commitment to his proposal. In making explicit the conflict between managerialism and professionalism, Remy would make the culture of compliance explicit, and no doubt provoke discomfort all round. But next time anyone said 'forget that college nonsense', he would ask whether they wanted him to forget about the injustice too.

So, what can we do when an unhelpful organizational culture stands in the way of promoting a critically reflective approach?

Have your say

If you are unhappy about the effects of a managerialist culture on your organization and the services it provides, then volunteering, where possible, to sit on planning committees and working parties can give you the opportunity to give your perspective on key matters, and also to argue for the voices of those we serve to be heard. While a diversity of interests can inhibit change, such involvement can provide a platform for differing perspectives to be heard and competing concerns appreciated.

Seek out like-minded people

Organizations are powerful entities and, while a lone voice can sometimes make a difference, a collective one can be much more effective. It can therefore pay dividends to make alliances with others who share your concern that a reflective approach is devalued in your workplace. Professional organizations tend to put up a fight when the principles on which a profession is built come under challenge and are therefore a potential source of support when trying to foster a culture of learning.

Use the right channels

When feeling demoralized it can be very tempting to have a good 'moan' amongst ourselves, but this rarely achieves anything positive and often just reinforces low morale where it exists. If our aim is to challenge an organizational culture that devalues what we value, then that challenge, if it is to have any chance of success, needs to be:

■ targeted at those who have the power to make changes at that level; and
■ presented as clear and constructive commentary that spells out what we object to and why.

Revisit professional values

It can be very heartening to remind ourselves of why we chose to work with people in the way we do as part of a commitment to our profession's aims. This can serve as a boost to morale and energize us to keep on trying to resist the pressure to work in situations where there is a danger that working practices, or the sheer volume of input expected of us, will compromise those values.

And finally, if we cannot change an anti-intellectual culture, then there is a lot to be said for ignoring it and continuing to plough our own furrow, as it were. If there is an expectation that we work in a bureaucratic way that compromises our professional principles and trivializes a reflective approach, then we can tell ourselves, 'I'm better than that!' and make sure that we do not allow what is happening around us to dampen our own enthusiasm or negatively affect our own practice.

Voice of experience 6.2

Some of my colleagues are very negative about the registration requirements that have been introduced to monitor standards in our profession. But these requirements have given me just what I need to fight what I see as a threat to our value base. I can't meet efficiency targets without compromising the anti-discriminatory principles which underpin my profession. Now that I have to demonstrate that I am adhering to a code of professional behaviour in order to retain my professional title, I can cite this when I am asked to work in a manner that compromises a reflective approach.

Alex, a resource centre manager

A LACK OF APPROPRIATE SKILLS

High-quality reflective practice is a highly skilled activity. It involves a wide range of skills, some of which we will have built up as part of our general education and life experience. However, other skills may need to be consciously worked on over time to build them up (indeed, this is part of reflective practice – concentrating explicitly on what needs to change and develop). Someone who lacks the necessary skills may therefore struggle with developing reflective practice. Such skills would include:

- **Analytical skills**. Being able to identify key issues and recognize patterns and interconnections are important parts of being reflective. It involves translating what can be very confusing, complex situations into relatively ordered and meaningful understandings of what is happening and what needs to happen.
- **Self-awareness skills**. Being able to appreciate what impact we are having on the situations we are dealing with and what impact those situations are having on us is what self-awareness is all about. Some people find this relatively easy, while others may find it difficult to develop the insights involved. Explicitly focusing on these issues will enable us to develop our skills over time, especially if we are able to secure appropriate support from sources we can trust.
- **Critical thinking**. This involves being able to see beneath the surface, to recognize the underlying reasoning and assumptions (the depth), as well as processes and dynamics that relate to power relations and the potential for discrimination and oppression to occur (the breadth). In some respects, this involves 'unlearning' what our socialization has taught us, as our upbringing will have involved taking certain issues for granted (the respective roles of men and women, for example).
- **Communication skills**. Reflective practice does not have to be a solitary activity. As we noted in Chapter 3, there is a lot of value in the shared learning that can arise from one-to-one or 'dyadic' reflection (supervision, mentoring or coaching, for example) or group reflection (training courses, team development sessions, learning sets and so on). Being able to communicate effectively in such settings will be an important part of making them a success and an effective use of our time. While we all have basic communication skills, the skills used in shared reflection may need to be at a more advanced level.

This is not an exhaustive list of skills, but should be enough to paint a picture of just how skilled an activity reflection is. If we are lacking any of these skills or do not have them at a suitably advanced level, then we may struggle to make the most of our opportunities to develop reflective practice. However, this is not a cause for pessimism or defeatism. Skills, by their very nature, can be developed through practice. It is also possible to learn from others, to be able to see how they handle situations, for example, or to seek guidance from them.

Another possible scenario is that we may have the skills, but do not recognize that we have them. We may be so used to utilizing one or more of the skills that we are oblivious to the fact that we are operating in a particular way, drawing on particular skills in the process. This then adds further emphasis to the point made above about the importance of self-awareness, as part of this can be developing a clear picture of our strengths (so that we can build on them) and our weaknesses (so that we can build them up and, ideally, turn them into strengths).

Perhaps the most significant point to emphasize in relation to this particular obstacle is that we should not underestimate the skills involved in reflective practice, nor should we allow ourselves to underestimate our abilities to develop those skills over time, provided that we receive the appropriate support.

When it comes to addressing problems of a lack of skills, the following strategies should prove helpful:

Take the initiative

Given that we need to be proficient in a number of skills in order to practise reflectively, it can pay dividends to do a 'skills audit' on ourselves, so that we can work out where we need to acquire new skills or improve those we already have. Whether we do so through our own reading, attending training courses or taking advice from colleagues, it is important to remember that the learning needs to take place in the context of how these skills will help us to practise reflectively. The material may not be presented with this in mind, and so we need to make those links for ourselves if a more informed and reflective practice is our goal.

Claim 'me' time

Where a skill deficit is proving to be an obstacle, this can be raised with line managers as a learning need. After all, employers have a duty to ensure that employees have the skills needed to do the job they are employed to do. In most situations, asking for 'time out' or study time to develop the skills that underpin reflective practice would not seem to be unreasonable, in our eyes.

Seek out a mentor

Although we may feel reluctant to express what we consider to be inadequacies, more skilled colleagues can be an invaluable source of support and guidance. We would stress here that the key word is *skilled*, rather than experienced, because the most experienced colleague may not necessarily be the most skilled – it could just be that he or she has been 'winging it' for longer! We would suggest looking for support from those who seem to know what they are doing and have critical awareness, regardless of the length of time they have been around.

And, finally, we need to remember that we are all 'works in progress'. When we become qualified and registered professionals, our certificates and diplomas indicate that we have the skills necessary to practise at a *beginning* level in our chosen field. Taking responsibility for our own ongoing learning is one of the bedrocks of critically reflective practice, and so we should see skills development as a positive goal, rather than as an obstacle to be overcome.

ANXIETY, FEAR OR LOW CONFIDENCE

One of the reasons an aspiring reflective practitioner may not have developed certain skills (or may not realize he or she has those skills) could be a lack of confidence. This, in turn, may arise from certain anxieties or fears relating to those skills or the areas where they are expected to be put into practice. Indeed, anxiety, fear or low confidence can in themselves be a significant barrier to developing reflective practice. Consider the following examples:

> ■ **Using professional knowledge**. One of the important aspects of reflective practice that was discussed earlier is the process of *surfacing* or making the implicit explicit, particularly in relation to the professional knowledge base we are drawing upon. This can lead to concerns on the part of some people who may feel worried about surfacing an inadequate or out-of-date knowledge base – that is, they may feel that this process will reveal embarrassing gaps in their knowledge base. Consequently, they would

prefer the risks involved in 'winging it' to the relative certainties of being exposed as someone whose knowledge is wanting. There are, of course, two main problems with this approach: (i) *everyone* will have gaps in their knowledge base; it is unrealistic to expect anyone to have a complete grasp of the underpinning knowledge of a particular profession or discipline – especially as that knowledge base will grow and change over time; (ii) if we are not honest about the gaps and thus our learning needs, then we will not be open to learning – there is a very real danger that we will get stuck in a rut and not grow and develop over time.

- **Taking risks**. There are also the wider anxieties of taking risks. Some people may prefer to stay in their 'comfort zone' – that is, they may be unwilling to stretch themselves, enter new territory or try out new ideas or approaches. This will not only reduce their effectiveness by unnecessarily restricting the repertoire of steps they can take to make progress, it will also mean that they will not grow and develop over time – that is, it will become another obstacle to learning. Being prepared to go outside our comfort zone is therefore an important underpinning of reflective practice. This does not mean that we should be reckless or expose ourselves to unnecessary risks, but it does mean that we should not allow ourselves to become trapped in a narrow, 'safe' or 'cosy' approach to our work, as this clearly involves doing a serious disservice to the people we are tying to help or support.

- **Exposure to criticism**. There will be few if any people who enjoy being criticized, particularly where such criticism is unfair or unwarranted. It is therefore understandable that many people will be very careful and cautious in trying to make sure that their work is not open to scrutiny. However, not being comfortable with being open to challenge can be a costly business in so far as it can mean (i) we close off opportunities to learn from constructive and helpful criticism; (ii) we do not take the opportunity of how to respond appropriately to unfair criticism; (iii) there may be errors or false assumptions in our work that go undetected, possibly with disastrous consequences in some situations; and (iv) not being open to challenge can undermine both our professional credibility (that is, how much faith others have in us as competent professionals) and our ability to work in partnership – especially if our unwillingness to be challenged makes us come across as arrogant, dogmatic or not open minded. If criticism is offered constructively and appropriately, we should have the good grace to seek to learn from it. If it is offered

destructively or inappropriately, we should have the courage to
challenge it. But simply avoiding criticism, scrutiny or challenge is
a much more dangerous path to follow.

■ **Role anxiety**. Some people may experience a degree of discomfort with using techniques and tools as frameworks for promoting reflective practice (see Chapter 4). For example, it is not
uncommon for some people to argue, when being introduced to
reflective practice tools and techniques (on a training course,
perhaps), that: 'I am a practitioner. I'm not sure I would feel
comfortable using training tools like these – I don't have a background or interest in providing training.' Of course, this is based
on a misunderstanding, as the tools and techniques available,
while often applicable in a training and development context, are
not limited to that context. They are tools for reflection and
learning and can be used just as effectively in a practice (or
management) context as in a training room. We should therefore not allow this type of misunderstanding to prevent us from
making use of some very valuable tools for reflective practice.

It is understandable that anxiety, fear or low confidence can stand in the way
of reflective practice. However, given the importance of reflective practice and
the dangers of practising in a non-reflective way, it is important that we have
the courage to address our anxieties and fears as best we can (with the support
of others where possible), and have enough faith in ourselves to tackle the
'demons' of low self-confidence and self-doubt.

Tackling these demons can be done, in part, by means of the following.

Turn negative influences to positive

Where anxiety becomes an obstacle to progress it can set in motion a vicious
circle where the anxiety saps confidence and the low confidence then feeds
back into and reinforces that anxiety. Trying to change the nature of that
process can therefore be a worthwhile strategy to work on. If we think in
terms of the benefits that practising reflectively can bring – the feeling of being
in control, knowing what we are trying to achieve, feeling positive about our
roles, and so on – we can see that it is possible to turn the process around and
into a virtuous circle (that is, the opposite of a vicious circle: one that goes

from strength to strength), whereby practising reflectively helps to make us feel more confident, which then serves to overcome or at least minimize the anxiety. This will not happen by wishful thinking, though, and we need to make that first step outside of our comfort zone if we are to break the vicious circle and set a virtuous one in motion.

Pat ourselves on the back

We have referred earlier to the fact that working in an 'anti-learning' culture can have a negative effect on confidence and commitment. It is therefore important that we do our utmost to resist cultural norms that hinder rather than help. For example, if the work culture is one in which comments such as 'We're all about practice here' or 'Forget about what they told you on your course, you're in the real world now' tend to go unchallenged, it becomes even more important to take pride in being a reflective practitioner and see learning as an essential component of critically reflective practice. It is easy to become demoralized in an environment where people are dismissive of what we see as fundamental to good practice. We recognize that this can put a strain on energy and morale, but like-minded people can be invaluable allies in reinforcing our belief in ourselves and our capacity to make a positive difference in people's lives.

Authenticity

Being authentic means being true to ourselves and not trying to find excuses elsewhere. In effect, it means taking responsibility for ourselves, taking ownership of our actions. If we want to tackle what is getting in the way of progress, we need to engage in a process of critical self-reflection in order to locate where the power to move forward with that aim lies. It is all too easy to blame those factors that are contributing to our fear or anxiety about reflective practice and use them as scapegoats to deflect away from ourselves the responsibility for addressing them. Some things are within our power to change, others we can only influence but, even where obstacles are not of our own making, there is always something we can do, even if that means moving out of a demoralizing environment and applying for a post where our own commitment to reflective practice is shared by our employer.

Practice focus 6.3
While preparing for an appraisal session Joan's manager, Safiya, realized that she never put herself forward for a place on training courses, nor did she interact very much with students or other visitors to the team. This struck her as odd, because she had always thought of Joan as a competent member of the team with a wealth of experience. When she broached the issue of Joan acting as a mentor to a newly qualified worker, Joan's reluctance prompted her to ask why she appeared to be so uncomfortable with the idea. It soon became apparent that Joan felt threatened by those who had qualified more recently than she had, and that she would not be able to 'hold her own' in discussions about theory. Safiya wondered whether Joan was conceptualizing the worlds of theory and practice as two separate spheres and persuaded her to attend a reflective practice workshop where she knew that the integration of the two concepts would be the major theme. This proved to be a turning point for Joan in terms of her understanding and also her confidence in her ability as a learner herself, and as someone who could contribute to the learning of others. She proved to be popular as a mentor because of her enthusiasm and commitment to making the learning journey a shared one, and was no longer 'afraid' of theory. She had come to realize that her practice had always been informed by a theory base, and that sharing her knowledge and insight with others was an excellent way to make sure that this continued to be the case.

MISUNDERSTANDING THE NATURE OF REFLECTIVE PRACTICE

In Chapter 1, the point was made that there are various myths about reflective practice that can get in the way of its development. The prevalence of these myths can lead to a situation in which some people have a very superficial or misleading understanding of what is involved, and this in turn can lead to a situation in which reflective practice is blocked – prevented from developing by a failure to appreciate what it is really about. For example, some people seem to think that reflective practice is simply a matter of pausing for thought from time to time. They will therefore not appreciate what is involved in terms of, for example, connecting reflection-in-action and reflection-on-action or of making links between both them of them and the underlying professional knowledge base.

Another aspect of this problem is when people are called upon to provide reflective accounts (for example, as part of a portfolio of evidence for an educational qualification – see Chapter 5), but do not appreciate the difference between a descriptive account and a reflective or analytical one. In this way, they fail to get the benefit of having a genuinely reflective account to review and learn from.

Furthermore, the point was made in Chapter 1 that it is important to distinguish between an open knowledge base (that is, one that is open to scrutiny and which can grow and develop over time) and a closed one (an implicit knowledge base that is not open to challenge or development). Some people reflect on their practice, but without engaging with an open knowledge base, in the sense that they may identify the assumptions on which their work is based, but not go the necessary step further to question those assumptions, to subject them to critical scrutiny and to link them to other aspects of the knowledge base.

This significant obstacle emphasizes the importance of having a good foundation of understanding of reflective practice and not making do with a superficial or distorted perspective. In terms of tackling this obstacle, then, what needs to be achieved is a clearer understanding of what reflective practice actually involves. For you personally, it is to be hoped that this book will have done enough to ensure that you have a clear understanding of the nature of critically reflective practice. However, when it comes to trying to make sure that others do not labour under any misapprehensions of what reflective practice is all about, the following may be helpful.

Team or staff meetings

You could consider raising the issues at a staff or team meeting – especially if some of these meetings are designated as staff development sessions. You could perhaps find a suitable article or book chapter to photocopy and use as a handout to form the basis of discussion. Alternatively, if you feel confident enough (or you have a knowledgeable colleague who feels confident enough), you could arrange for a presentation to be made to the team or staff group on the benefits of critically reflective practice and the dangers and costs of uncritical, non-reflective practice.

Training courses

It could be a worthwhile use of your time to try and find out whether there are any courses on reflective practice available within your organization. If not, perhaps there are open courses not too far away and possibly the funding available to purchase one or more places on one of them. If neither is available, it may be worth contacting your organization's training department to encourage them to provide or commission appropriate training on this important subject.

Leading by example

The point was made earlier that, if we cannot change an unhelpful culture that is preventing the development of reflective practice, then at least we can ignore that culture and make sure that our own actions are not unduly influenced by it. In doing so, this gives us the opportunity to lead by example. If we make sure that our actions are consistent with critically reflective practice and show others how helpful this is in terms of, for example, avoiding the development of stress (through a sense of a lack of control combined with low morale) and achieving high levels of professional practice, then we can play a significant part as role models.

Student placements

If your team or staff group play host to students on placement from time to time, then this may be a useful opportunity for raising awareness of what critically reflective practice is all about. For example, it may be possible to have one or more students involved in a project relating to critical reflection that can help to raise awareness, to a limited extent at least, throughout the organization and, in the process, seek to clear up some of the common misunderstandings (as outlined in Chapter 1). Some students may not feel comfortable with this type of project, whereas others may very much welcome the challenge.

Good management

If you are a manager and misunderstanding amongst your team members is the barrier, then you should find it helpful to encourage them to read, discuss and get to know what the task is and what it is not – recognizing that *informed* practice is at the root of developing reflective practice. This can be done through supervision (dyadic reflective space), through, as mentioned above, team meetings (group reflective space) and in whatever ways present themselves over time.

CONCLUSION

This chapter has explored a range of obstacles that can stand in the way of developing critically reflective practice and provided some suggestions as to how these can be dealt with. Consistent with the philosophy of reflective practice, we offer no simple definitive answers, but rather, more realistically, some points of guidance to act as food for thought to encourage further development.

A key theme has been that we can be significantly helped in overcoming obstacles to critically reflective practice by reaffirming ourselves as professionals – that is, not just as bureaucrats who mindlessly follow procedure (Payne, 2000), but rather as individuals who have a knowledge base and a set of values to draw upon in wrestling with the complexities of the demands of working in the helping professions. We have known for some time that simply following procedures is not a workable response in the helping professions. This is because the work involves working with *people,* and therefore incorporates a significant degree of uncertainty and unpredictability.

Working with uncertainty creates a need to tailor responses to the specific circumstances, and does not fit comfortably with working in routinized, uncritical ways. It is therefore essential that we are able to overcome the barriers, rather than give up and sink into defeatism. It will not always be an easy journey, but the obstacles we encounter are not insurmountable if the commitment to good practice is strong enough to see us through.

This chapter, we hope, has gone some way towards establishing a foundation from which you can develop a better understanding of the barriers we are likely to encounter (the ones discussed here plus others that are likely to arise) and some ideas and insights about how we can rise to the challenge of removing or avoiding those barriers or, at least, minimizing their impact.

Chapter 7

Conclusion:
Rising to the Challenge

INTRODUCTION

In this final chapter we summarize the main arguments we have put forward and present our views on how best we can, individually and collectively, rise to the challenge of developing critically reflective practice in circumstances where, on the one hand, we have considerable misunderstanding and over-simplification of what it is all about and, on the other, strong resistance to making it a reality – for example, through organizational cultures that encourage staff (and managers) to 'just get on with the job'.

What we have tried to do in this book is to steer a positive and constructive path in between these two destructive extremes. In terms of the oversimplifications and superficial understandings, we have tried to show the complexities involved and have suggested some ways in which these can be addressed. In terms of the difficulties we face in relation to resistance and obstacles, we have tried to be of assistance by highlighting some of the main problems involved and, once again, suggested some possible ways forward.

In doing so we have made every effort to blend theory and practice successfully and helpfully. In terms of theory, we have tried to do justice to the complexities involved without this becoming an advanced-level theoretical treatise. We see no problem with such an advanced-level treatise, but recognize that that is not what this book is about. In terms of practice, we have tried to provide helpful guidance, but without being prescriptive or giving the impression that simple, off-the-peg solutions have any value. If we had fallen into such a trap, we would have been undermining the whole tenor of the book, as it is clearly a key part of the philosophy of reflective practice to recognize that each situation needs to be dealt with on its own merits and not in standardized ways – the reflective practitioner cuts the cloth of knowledge, values and experience to suit the circumstances of the practice situation being dealt with.

What remains for us to do now is to pull together our views about how to respond to the challenge of making critically reflective practice a reality (or, more of a reality than it is now). We do this by highlighting seven sets of issues that we feel are crucial underpinnings of what we are trying to achieve. We shall conclude, then, by summarizing our views on each of these seven areas in turn.

THINKING

A career in the helping professions is likely to be a demanding one, with a great deal of pressure involved. It is understandable, then, that people will be tempted to press on with *doing* their work and devote relatively little time to *thinking* about the work. However, we have seen that this can be a dangerous temptation, as it means that we can be practising without really understanding what we are doing and why we are doing it. We can fall foul of 'mindless' practice, rather than gain the benefits of an informed and mindful approach that allows us to:

- Draw on our extensive professional knowledge base.
- Be aware of potential pitfalls and dangers.
- Develop a good understanding of the complex situations we are dealing with.
- Be creative and not simply rely on habit and routine.
- Tailor solutions to the specific circumstances rather than deal with them in standardized ways.
- Be in a position to justify our actions if called upon to do so.

Adopting such an approach will, in turn give us:

- A greater sense of control and thus make us less prone to stress.

- A higher level of confidence based on the fact that we are able to practise at a more advanced level.
- More job satisfaction and thus a higher level of motivation and morale.
- A spur to learning and thus a solid foundation for continuous professional development.
- Greater professional credibility in the eyes of those we serve and of fellow professionals within the multidisciplinary network.

What it amounts to is avoiding BOB (the Bypassing Our Brain problem – an easy trap to fall into when we are busy and perhaps tired). Reflective practice does not mean that we must be concentrating fully at all times – that would be an unrealistic expectation – but it does mean that we should make every effort not to slide into a dangerous, unthinking and routinized approach, no matter how much pressure we are under.

But, reflective practice is not simply a matter of thinking in a general, unstructured way. It is more complex that this. Bruner (1996) argues that reflection is: 'a process of sense making, of going "meta," turning round on what one has learned through bare experience, thinking about thinking' (p. 10, cited in Lyons, 2004, p. 37). 'Meta' is the Greek word for 'above', and so 'going meta' means getting an overview of the situation and our thinking about it (closely linked to the holistic approach referred to earlier as 'helicopter vision'). Reflective practice is therefore more than 'just having a little think' every now and again. It involves having a focused, mindful approach to our work and the rationale for our actions.

A thoughtful, reflective approach should also make it easier for us to keep high-quality records of our work (an important aspect of professional accountability). This is because it is difficult (if not impossible) to write clearly if we are not thinking clearly. High-quality professional records therefore depend on a degree of clarity of thinking – and, as we have seen, clarity and focus are important elements of reflective practice.

The other side of the coin is to make sure that the quality of our thinking is reflected in our writing. That is, it is possible to have clear thinking that is not apparent in the quality of the records. It is a pity when this occurs, as it means that we are not doing justice to the quality of our practice. It also means that others who may rely on our records in future may not benefit from the high-quality groundwork we have done.

THINKING CRITICALLY

Our argument throughout the book has clearly been that a thoughtful, reflective, well-informed approach is far preferable to an unthinking approach based on habit, routine, knee-jerk responses or simply copying others. However, we have also argued that our thoughtful, reflective approach needs to be a *critically* reflective approach – that is, it needs to be consistent with:

> ■ **Critical depth**. This involves being able to identify underlying arguments and assumptions (which may be false, distorted or otherwise inappropriate). It is geared towards making sure that (i) our own thinking is not flawed and thereby potentially dangerously misleading; and (ii) we are not seduced by the flawed thinking of others.
>
> ■ **Critical breadth**. Professional practice can easily become 'atomistic' – that is, too individually focused and thus neglectful of the wider social and political context of our practice (and indeed of the lives of the people we serve). Critically reflective practice therefore takes account of power relations and related processes of discrimination, stigmatization and exclusion.

In relation to the breadth aspect, Fook makes an important point in arguing that:

> A critical reflective approach should allow . . . workers to interact with and respond to power dynamics in situations in a much more flexible, differentiated and therefore effective way. By making less 'blanket' assumptions about power, the critically reflective practitioner should be able to engage with the specific power dynamics of situations in more relevant and effective ways.
>
> (2002, p. 157)

It would be naïve to assume that our professional actions do not involve power dynamics (Thompson, 2007). It can be dangerous not to be tuned in to such power issues – dangerous because:

■   We may not spot the significance of discrimination in people's lives, and may thus do them a considerable disservice in failing to take account of such potentially crucial aspects of their circumstances.

■   We may actually reinforce such discrimination, albeit unwittingly, and thus increase the levels of oppression, disadvantage and distress, rather than reduce them. We thus become part of the problem, rather than part of the solution.

It is therefore essential that our practice is tuned in to such issues, that our reflection has this critical breadth. Without this, we could be hindering rather than helping.

In terms of the depth element, we are not expected to be experts in formal logic, but we would be very wise to take whatever reasonable steps we can to develop our understanding and skills in relation to recognizing, for example, the difference between a valid argument and a spurious one. This is something that you may find difficult at first, but it is a skill that can be developed over time. It is also something that does not have to be tackled alone. We can help each other develop our skills in this area. Returning to our discussions in Chapter 3 of the different contexts of practice, critical analysis skills can be fostered through dyadic reflective space (for example, supervision, mentoring or coaching) and/or group reflective space (training courses may be available in some areas around these issues).

We have presented the breadth and depth elements as different aspects of critically reflective practice, but it is also important to recognize that there are interconnections between them. For example, the reason an argument or assumption may be flawed or distorted may be that it is being used to shore up a particular ideological position. It may be, perhaps, that unquestioned assumptions (depth) about male and female roles in society (breadth) are underpinning an individual's reasoning about a situation. The reason they are making these assumptions is that they subscribe to a value base that does not include a commitment to gender equality. Once we realize this, we can start to see why, from the value base of the helping professions, with its emphasis on the importance of equality and diversity, the assumptions they are making need to be challenged.

In effect, critically reflective practice involves not taking things at face value and therefore questioning the underpinning assumptions and broader processes that will be shaping the situations we deal with.

BEING SELF-AWARE

Just as work pressures can, if we let them, prevent us from adopting a thoughtful, reflective approach that enables us to draw on our professional knowledge base, workload demands can also prevent us from adopting a self-aware approach that enables us to draw on our experience and character. Work pressures can lead us into losing sight of who we are, what impact we are having on the situations we are dealing with and what impact they are having on us. In the helping professions, it is often the human element that makes the difference, the ways in which we, as individuals, can bring our own experiences and insights to bear, our personal warmth, empathy and concern.

This does not mean that, say, the reassurance and personal connection a nurse offers is more important than the medication given, but it does mean that the absence of the former could be just as significant as the absence of the latter. However, if we adopt an unthinking, non-reflective approach to our work, then we may find that this human dimension slips away, with the result that people experience our efforts to help as mechanistic and dehumanizing – once again, we run the risk of being part of the problem, rather than part of the solution.

Reflective practice involves being able to tune in to the specific circum-stances we are dealing with and not simply applying a standardized or blanket approach to practice. To be able to do that we need a degree of sensitivity, the ability to identify the subtleties involved in terms of what is happening, what processes are contributing to what is happening and the implications of what is unfolding. We will, of course, be part of that unfolding – we will be part of the 'dynamic' that is shaping the situation and how it develops. We are not neutral, invisible and silent observers of the practice situations we encounter – we become part of them. We can play a part in improving the situation – working towards positive, valued outcomes – or we can be instrumental in the situation getting worse and resulting in negative, undesirable outcomes. If we are not sensitive to the part we play, to how we influence the unfolding of events, we place ourselves in a doubly dangerous situation. First, it can be dangerous in terms of the harm that we can do to the people we are seeking to help and, second, it can be dangerous in terms of our own credibility in the short term and our overall career development in the longer term. Given the important part we play in the situations we are involved with, self-awareness becomes an essential foundation of good practice.

Self-awareness involves recognizing that we are not infallible, that we will make mistakes from time to time. Self-awareness therefore involves a degree of humility and the recognition of the dangers of being too self-assured or overconfident. Self-awareness, then, should prevent us from adopting too fixed and dogmatic a view of the situations we deal with. Taylor and White warn of the dangers of a complacent approach that lacks such awareness:

> armed with the comfortable belief that they have sure and certain knowledge, health and welfare professionals may be less likely to reflect appropriately on their judgements and decision making, thus making error more, rather than less, likely. Health and welfare professionals need to acknowledge the uncertainty, ambiguity and complexity that lie at the heart of their practice (Parton 1999).
>
> (2000, p. 5)

Self-awareness, then, as part of critically reflective practice, has an important part to play in making sure that we do not become too inflexible in our approach. The flexibility of being able to tailor solutions to specific circumstances is, of course, at the heart of reflective practice.

As we noted in Chapter 1, individuals do not exist in a social vacuum. Being self-aware therefore needs to incorporate being *socially* aware, attuned to the wider contexts in which we work. In this way, self-awareness makes a positive contribution to the *critical* element of reflective practice, based on having an awareness of, and sensitivity to, the role of power relations, inequality and disadvantage in shaping the problems that form the bedrock of our work in the helping professions. Fook captures this point well:

> Reframing our practice as contextual therefore means we reframe our practice as working *with* environments, rather than working *despite* environments. We see ourselves as part of a context, ourselves responsible for aspects of that context. In this way, we see possibilities for change, for *creating different microclimates within broader contexts.*
>
> (2002, p. 162)

Self-awareness therefore needs to involve awareness of the social contexts in which we operate. Self-awareness is one of the foundation stones of critically reflective practice and, in turn, critically reflective practice supports and facilitates the development of greater self-awareness.

CAPITALIZING ON LEARNING

Every day we are presented with opportunities for learning: situations that enable us to practise and develop our skills; new information to develop our knowledge base; new experiences to learn lessons from (both the successes and the failures); challenges to our assumptions and ways of thinking that spur us to review and develop our approach; and opportunities to learn from others (through direct observation/co-working, discussion and/or reading). However, a combination of workplace pressures and an unthinking approach can mean that we miss a great many of these opportunities. As Clutterbuck confirms:

> The result is that many people spend most of their working lives missing opportunities to learn. It is not just the workshop we could not attend, or the book we did not read, or the challenging project we did not put our name forward for. It is the continuous failure to tap into the views, perspective and knowledge of the people around us.
>
> (1998, p. 14)

It is a great pity that so many people miss out on these opportunities for learning, and thereby fail to gain the benefits that accrue from continuous professional development: enhanced levels of understanding that can lead to enhanced levels of practice; greater confidence that comes from being better informed and better equipped; and so on.

But it does not have to be this way. By having a more 'switched on' approach to what is going on around us, we can significantly increase the chances of making the most of the learning opportunities that present themselves to us on a more or less daily basis. Reflective practice can help us to have this more 'switched on' approach, more tuned in to what is going on around us – especially the learning opportunities presented. Indeed, reflective practice could be seen as *learning* practice, in the sense that a reflective approach helps us to learn, and being tuned in to learning will support the development of critically reflective practice.

We can capitalize on learning in a number of ways, linked to the three contexts of reflection discussed in Chapter 3:

■ **Personal reflective space**. This can be linked to the discussion above of self-awareness (and social awareness), where the value of being more alert to our part in the situations we deal with was emphasized. The same process of awareness can be used as the basis of learning. We can ask ourselves: What can I learn from this situation? What new knowledge or skills are involved? How can this situation help me develop my existing knowledge and skills? Does this situation tell me anything about values?

■ **Dyadic reflective space**. One-to-one situations, such as super-vision, mentoring and coaching can be invaluable opportunities for learning – for example, by reviewing our practice and drawing out the learning from it; by integrating theory and prac-tice and so on. A skilled supervisor, mentor, coach, practice teacher or tutor can be extremely helpful in supporting learning. We should therefore make sure that, as far as possible, we make the most of the learning that can be gained from using such support to the full.

■ **Group reflective space**. Training courses and other group learning experiences can be a more or less complete waste of time, or they can be extremely stimulating, rewarding and fruitful learning experiences that broaden, deepen and reaffirm our knowledge base, extend and strengthen our skills base and provide a basis for examining and exploring our value base. They can boost confidence, increase motivation and provide valuable food for thought about how to develop our practice. Whether the event is predominantly negative or predominantly positive will depend in part on the other participants and the event leader, but our own part in the proceedings will also be crucial. How much effort and concentration we put in, whether we do any preparatory work beforehand and whether we make the effort to transfer the learning to our practice (with or without the help of a supervisor or mentor) after the event will all be significant factors in determining whether or not we are able to make the most of the learning potential on offer.

Capitalizing on learning has huge benefits for relatively little investment of time and effort. What is crucial, though, is having a positive mindset that is geared towards learning, one that sees the value of growth and development and involves a commitment to drawing out the lessons to be learned from the work we do.

SUPPORTING OTHERS

At various points we have made it clear that developing reflective practice is not something we have to do alone. There is much to be gained from supporting one another and collaborating in whatever ways we can to make critically reflective practice a reality as a fundamental underpinning to our work.

It is undoubtedly the case that much of our educational system is based on competition (who is going to get the highest grades?) and, while that may arguably have some value, the price we pay for it is that so many people associate learning with competition, rather than cooperation and collaboration. To maximize the potential of reflective practice, we therefore need to place the emphasis on collaboration (working in partnership) rather than competition.

But, this is not just an individual responsibility. Organizations too have some degree of responsibility for trying to ensure that learning and reflection are encouraged and supported, and that these are seen as shared endeavours, rather than simply solo projects. Clutterbuck supports this view:

> One of the aims for the organisation of the early twenty-first century must be to create a climate of development where helping others to learn is natural, expected – and hopefully – quite unremarkable. That will not happen with current piecemeal approaches. It is time that the learning alliance took its place alongside more formal approaches to learning, as a fundamental driver of business and personal change.
>
> (1998, p. 134)

The term 'learning alliance' refers to the dyadic reflective space discussed earlier. Clutterbuck sees this as central to organizational learning. We would agree, but would also want to emphasize the broader role of leadership. While individual employees can play a significant part and so too can supervisors and managers, there is also the role of the organizations' leaders to consider. Leadership is about shaping the culture of the organization and motivating staff and managers to fulfil the organization's goals. If we apply this to critically reflective practice, we can see that leaders have great potential for shaping a culture that is supportive of learning and reflection and creating a spirit of collaboration in that direction.

BEING PROFESSIONAL

Working in an uncritical, non-reflective way is a pretty poor basis for professional practice. Being professional involves drawing on professional knowledge and value bases and having professional accountability. Each of these is very relevant when it comes to critically reflective practice. We shall consider each of them in turn.

Drawing on a professional knowledge base

Central to the notion of reflective practice is the idea that it is *informed* practice – that is, it is rooted in a professional knowledge base, rather than just guesswork, habit or prejudice. In particular, it is important that this knowledge base should be, as far as possible, an *open* knowledge base – that is, one that is open to scrutiny and challenge (and is therefore not dogmatic) and can grow and develop over time.

This means being able to integrate theory and practice: making sure that practice is informed by theoretical understanding and theory is tested by practice. Lovelock, Lyons and Powell make reference to: 'Lang's elegant notion of making theory "lived practice" and practice "lived theory"' (2004, p. 177). It is important that we do not return to the days of theory and practice being seen as separate, largely unconnected domains, as such a short-sighted approach fails to recognize how valuable theoretical insights can be for making sense of practice and how valuable practice can be for testing and extending theory.

A common misunderstanding is that theory 'belongs' to academics in universities, while practice 'belongs' to practitioners in the field. The reality is that theory belongs as much to practitioners as it does to academics. While university-based staff may well play an important role in teaching and, to a certain extent, developing theory, practitioners are daily using theory (if not always recognizing that they are) and also, to a certain extent, playing a part in developing theory (by putting it to test and perhaps by writing articles and even books about their use of theory in practice).

Drawing on a professional value base

Just as theory influences practice, often without our being aware of any direct linkages between the two, values are also strong influences on the work we do, the approach we take to it and how we perceive the situations we operate in. Our values provide an ethical foundation for our work – they give us a sense of what is right and what is wrong, acceptable or unacceptable.

Our value base will tend to incorporate traditional, well-established values, such as confidentiality and treating people with respect and dignity, as well as more contemporary values that have emerged relatively recently – for example, a commitment to equality and diversity. Reflective practice involves becoming more explicitly aware of our values, as it is only if we are aware of what they are that we can understand how they influence us. Also, having a more informed understanding of our value base puts us in a stronger position to deal with moral dilemmas, clashes of values and other such complications that are never far away in the helping professions.

Once we start to look more closely at values, we start to appreciate just how influential they are in shaping not only our thoughts and actions, but also our feelings. We neglect them at our peril. Critically reflective practice therefore needs to be attuned to the values dimension of professional practice and, indeed, of the wider sociopolitical context in which we work.

Respecting professional accountability

Part of our professional value base is the recognition that we are accountable for our actions – it would be entirely unethical to fail to take account of this responsibility. However, without reflective practice, accountability becomes a significant problem. This is because being accountable means that, at any point, we may be called to account for our actions (or inactions). To be in a position to do this with confidence involves having clarity about what we did and why we did it (the underlying rationale). We will struggle to do this if we have adopted an uncritical, non-reflective approach that simply involves standardized approaches and relying on routine and habit. To be able to justify our professional decision making, we need to be able to specify the process of thinking that informed the decision(s). If there was no real process of thinking, we will find ourselves defenceless if our practice is criticized in some way (as a result of a complaint, an inspection or litigation, for example).

By contrast, an informed, reflective approach puts us in a strong position to be able to justify why we acted in a particular way or adopted a particular approach to the case in hand. We will be able to say what influenced our decision making by reference to a professional knowledge base, a professional value base and a clearly worked out analysis of the situation. Even if, with hindsight, it turns out that we acted in error, it is likely that we will be respected for acting in good faith. However, if we make what turns out to be a valid decision purely by chance, and we are not therefore able to provide a professionally acceptable account of how we arrived at that decision, then we will be open to quite severe criticism and censure.

We are not recommending defensive practice. On the contrary, we are arguing that, if we practise reflectively and professionally, there is nothing to be defensive about.

MAKING PRACTICE WORK

We have presented critically reflective practice as a valuable approach to the demands of working in the helping professions. Our view is that is has excellent potential to be not only effective, but also rewarding and a basis for developing creative approaches. We shall discuss each of these aspects in turn.

Making practice effective

A participant on a reflective practice training course once remarked near the beginning of the day:

> I'm not sure if I'm going to find today useful. I'm quite a practical person. I have a job to do and I want to get on and do it. I don't see the point of navel gazing. That doesn't get the job done, does it? And that's what its' all about, isn't it – making a positive difference?

We would fully agree with the final point, but not with the premises on which it is based. This person seemed to be assuming that reflective practice is more akin to navel gazing than to providing a firm foundation for informed and effective practice. At the end of the day she apologized to the trainer and said she had previously completely misunderstood what reflective practice was all about. She could now see that it was actually a very valuable approach that had much to offer. Reflective practice, then, is not an alternative to effectiveness, but rather a foundation for it.

Making practice rewarding

If we allow our working lives to become dominated by unthinking routines and habits, standardized responses and a more or less complete lack of imagination, then we should not be surprised to find that our work will be unrewarding and unfulfilling. We will struggle to find meaning or gain satisfaction in our work. Critically reflective practice, by contrast, offers us a stimulating and rewarding approach to our working lives. It offers us the chance for making a positive difference where we can; for learning, growth and development – not only while we 'learn the ropes' at the beginning of our career, but throughout it; and for developing new approaches, new ways of thinking and new understandings. It also offers a foundation for genuine collaboration with others. Routinized approaches cannot realistically form the basis of partnership working – habitualized responses and limited understanding are not really conducive to 'joined-up' thinking.

Making practice creative

'Necessity is the mother of invention' is a well-known adage. Being inventive is what creativity is all about. And so, the more pressurized we are and the greater the shortage of resources, the more inventive we need to be – the more important it becomes for us to be able to come up with imaginative solutions.

There is a great irony here, in so far as routinized and standardized practices can numb us and demotivate us so much that we find it difficult to be creative and, without being able to be creative, we become prone to falling into unthinking routines. What is also significant is that practices that lack creativity and imagination can lead to the development of a culture that does not value creative approaches – and then creativity becomes even more difficult for those affected by such a culture. In other words, it is very easy for creativity to be stifled by habit and routine, even though creativity can be the 'antidote' to the malaise of unthinking, non-reflective practice.

CONCLUSION

Critically reflective practice clearly presents a number of challenges. However, we hope that this book has: (i) shown that the benefits of adopting such an approach (and the dangers of not doing so) make it a worthwhile commitment of time, effort and energy; and (ii) given helpful guidance about how to move forward in making critically reflective practice a reality.

We see progress in this area as being dependent on four sets of factors:

- Developing a more in-depth understanding of critically reflective practice, its basis, applicability and value – Part 1 was devoted to laying a foundation for moving away from the superficial understanding of these issues that we commonly encounter.
- Being able to integrate the theory underpinning critically reflective practice with actual use of critical reflection – Part 2 was devoted to exploring how these important links can be made.
- Professionals taking responsibility, both individually and collectively, for building on these foundations over time.
- Managers and policymakers – indeed, leaders of all kinds – taking responsibility for developing and sustaining workplace cultures that recognize the value of a critically reflective approach and the significant dangers of a 'just get on with the job' mentality.

We hope that the ideas we have put forward will help in relation to each of these four areas. In particular, we hope that the seven themes we have built the book around will make a contribution to developing a platform for understanding critically reflective practice and making it a reality.

To conclude, then, we see becoming a critically reflective practitioner as being based on:

- **Thinking**. It is important to be able to draw on our analytical powers to make sense of the complex situations we encounter in practice and to draw on our professional knowledge base.
- **Critical thinking**. This involves (i) being able to look below the surface of presenting situations to recognize the significance of the arguments and assumptions on which it is based; and also (ii) being able to see the wider picture of how social and political factors shape individual circumstances.
- **Being self-aware**. We need to be able to recognize the impact we have on the situations we deal with, and how they have an impact on us. Being self-aware also involves being socially aware, again appreciating the 'big picture' of how individual factors are shaped by wider social and political issues.
- **Capitalizing on learning**. Critical reflection is a basis for learning. Equally, continuous learning is a foundation for critically reflective practice.
- **Supporting others**. There are various aspects of personal responsibility involved in developing critically reflective practice, but we are not alone in these matters. We need to support one another in making critical reflection a reality.
- **Being professional**. This involves drawing on a professional knowledge base and a professional value base, as well as respecting professional accountability.
- **Making practice work**. For this we need to make sure, as far as possible, that our work is effective, rewarding and creative.

Rising to the challenge of critically reflective practice is by no means easy or straightforward. However, we believe strongly that it is well worth the effort to do so – especially if we work together and support one another. We wish you well in rising to the challenge of not only becoming a critically reflective practitioner, but also remaining one, despite the many discouragements that will come your way in a world in which critical reflection is not given the value and appreciation it deserves.

Guide to Further Learning

SUGGESTIONS FOR FURTHER READING

Reflective practice generally

Benner, P., Hooper-Kyriakidis, P. and Stannard, D. (1999) *Clinical Wisdom and Interventions in Critical Care: A Thinking-in-Action Approach*, Philadelphia, Saunders.

Bolton, G. (2001) *Reflective Practice*, London, Paul Chapman.

Bulman, C. and Schutz, S. (eds) (2004) *Reflective Practice in Nursing*, 3rd edn, Oxford, Blackwell.

Fook, J., Ryan, M. and Hawkins, L. (2000) *Professional Expertise: Practice, Theory and Education for Working in Uncertainty*, London, Whiting & Birch.

Dolan, P., Canavan, J. and Pinkerton, J. (eds) (2006) *Family Support as Reflective Practice*, London, Jessica Kingsley.

Fook, J. and Gardner, F. (2007), *Practising Critical Reflection: A Handbook*, Maidenhead, Open University Press

Gould, N. and Baldwin, M. (eds) (2004) *Social Work, Critical Reflection and the Learning Organization*, Aldershot, Ashgate.

Gould, N. and Taylor, I. (eds) (1996) *Reflective Learning for Social Work*, Aldershot, Arena.

Jasper, M. (2003) *Beginning Reflective Practice*, Cheltenham, Nelson Thornes.

Johns, C. (2004) *Becoming a Reflective Practitioner*, 2nd edn, Oxford, Blackwell.

Johns, C. and Freshwater, D. (eds) (2005) *Transforming Nursing Through Reflective Practice*, 2nd edn, Oxford, Blackwell.

Martyn, H. (ed.) (2000) *Developing Reflective Practice: Making Sense of Social Work in a World of Change*, Bristol, The Policy Press.

Osterman, K. F. and Kottkamp, R. B. (2004) *Reflective Practice for Educators*, 2nd edn, London, Sage.

Palmer, A., Burns, S. and Bulman, C. (eds) (1994), *Reflective Practice in Nursing: The Growth of the Reflective Practitioner*, Oxford, Blackwell Science.

Redmond, B. (2004) *Reflection in Action: Developing Reflective Practice in Health and Social Services*, Aldershot, Ashgate.

Rolfe, G., Freshwater, D. and Jasper, M. (2001) *Critical Reflection for Nursing and the Helping Professions*, Basingstoke, Palgrave Macmillan.

Schön, D. A. (1983) *The Reflective Practitioner: How Professionals Think in Action*, London, Temple Smith.

Taylor, B. (2006) *Reflective Practice: A Guide for Nurses and Midwives*, 2nd edn, Maidenhead, Open University Press.

Taylor, C. and White, S. (2000) *Practising Reflexivity in Health and Social Welfare: Making Knowledge*, Buckingham, Open University Press.

Thompson, N. (2006) *Promoting Workplace Learning*, Bristol, The Policy Press – see Chapter 3.

Theory and practice

Fook, J. (2002) *Social Work: Critical Theory and Practice*, London, Sage.

Lovelock, R., Lyons, K. and Powell, J. (eds) (2004) *Reflecting on Social Work: Discipline and Profession*, Aldershot, Ashgate.

Schön, D.A. (1983) *The Reflective Practitioner: How Professionals Think in Action*, London, Temple Smith.

Schön, D. A. (1992) 'The Crisis of Professional Knowledge and the Pursuit of an Epistemology of Practice', *Journal of Interprofessional Care*, 6(1).

Thompson, N. (2000) *Theory and Practice in Human Services*, Buckingham, Open University Press.

Thompson, N. (2006) *Promoting Workplace Learning*, Bristol, The Policy Press.

Evidence-based practice

Barratt, M. and Cooke, J. (2001) *Evidence-Based Practice*, Totnes, Dartington Hall Trust.

Humphries, B. (2003) 'What Else Counts as Evidence in Evidence-Based Social Work?', *Social Work Education*, 22(1).

Sheldon, B., and Chilvers, R. (2000) *Evidence-Based Social Care*, Lyme Regis, Russell House Publishing.

Trinder, L. and Reynolds, S. (eds) (2000) *Evidence-Based Practice: A Critical Approach*, Oxford, Blackwell.

Roberts, A. R. and Yeager, K. R. (eds) (2004) *Evidence-Based Practice Manual: Research and Outcome Measures in Health and Human Services*, Oxford, Oxford University Press.

Critical perspectives

Brechin, A., Brown, H. and Eby, M. A. (eds) (2000) *Critical Practice in Health and Social Care*, London, Sage.

Cottrell, S. (2005) *Critical Thinking Skills: Developing Effective Analysis and Argument*, Basingstoke, Palgrave Macmillan.

Christensen, T. (2001) *Wonder and Critical Reflection: An Invitation to Philosophy*, New Jersey/London, Prentice Hall.

Fook, J. (2002) *Social Work: Critical Theory and Practice*, London, Sage

Fook, J. and Gardner, F. (2007) *Practising Critical Reflection: A Handbook*, Maidenhead, Open University Press.

Murray, M. and Kujundzic, N. (2005) *Critical Reflection: A Textbook for Critical Thinking*, Montreal and Kingston/London, McGill-Queen's University Press.

Thompson, N. (2003) *Promoting Equality, Challenging Discrimination and Oppression*, 2nd edn, Basingstoke, Palgrave Macmillan.

Thompson, N. (2007) *Power and Empowerment*, Lyme Regis, Russell House Publishing.

Westwood, S. (2002) *Power and the Social*, London, Routledge.

White, S., Fook, J. and Gardner, F. (eds) (2006) *Critical Reflection in Health and Social Care*, Maidenhead, Open University Press.

The cognitive dimension

Bono, E. de (1990) *Lateral Thinking*, Harmondsworth, Penguin.

Bono, E. de (1991) *Practical Thinking*, 2nd edn, Harmondsworth, Penguin.

Bono, E. de (2000) *Six Thinking Hats*, Harmondsworth, Penguin.

Butterworth, J. and Thwaites, G. (2005) *Thinking Skills*, Cambridge, Cambridge University Press.

Christensen, T. (2001) *Wonder and Critical Reflection: An Invitation to Philosophy*, New Jersey/London, Prentice Hall.

Cottrell, S. (2005) *Critical Thinking Skills: Developing Effective Analysis and Argument*, Basingstoke, Palgrave Macmillan.

Hamer, M. (2006) *The Barefoot Helper: Mindfulness and Creativity in Social Work and the Helping Professions*, Lyme Regis, Russell House Publishing.

Murray, M. and Kujundzic, N. (2005) *Critical Reflection: A Textbook for Critical Thinking*, Montreal and Kingston/London, McGill-Queen's University Press.

Nelson-Jones, R. (1997) *Using Your Mind: Creative Thinking Skills for Work and Business Success*, London, Cassell.

The emotional dimension

Barbalet, J. (ed.) (2002) *Emotions and Sociology*, Oxford, Blackwell.

Bendelow, G. and Williams. S. J. (eds) (1998) *Emotions in Social Life: Critical Themes and Contemporary Issues*, London, Routledge.

Bolton, S. C. (2005) *Emotion Management in the Workplace*, Basingstoke, Palgrave Macmillan.

Cooper, R. and Sawaf, A. (1997) *Executive EQ: Emotional Intelligence in Business*, London, Orion Business.

Fineman, S. (ed.) (2000) *Emotion in Organizations*, 2nd edn, London, Sage.

Fischer, A. H. (ed.) (2000) *Gender and Emotion: Social Psychological Perspectives*, Cambridge, Cambridge University Press.

Goleman, D. (2004) *Destructive Emotions and How We Can Overcome Them: A Dialogue With the Dalai Lama*, London, Bloomsbury Publishing.

Goleman, D. (1996) *Emotional Intelligence: Why It Can Matter More Than IQ*, London, Bloomsbury Publishing.

Huffington, C., Armstrong, D., Halton, W., Hoyle, L. and Pooley, J. (eds) (2004) *Working Below the Surface: The Emotional Life of Contemporary Organizations*, London, Karnac.

Mervelede, P. E., Bridoux, D. and Vandamme, R. (2001) *7 Steps to Emotional Intelligence*, Carmarthen, Crown House Publishing.

Parkinson, B., Fischer, A. H. and Manstead, A. S. R. (2005) *Emotion in Social Relations: Cultural, Group and Interpersonal Processes*, Hove, Psychology Press.

Payne, R. L. and Cooper, C. L. (eds) (2001) *Emotions at Work: Theory, Research and Applications for Management*, Chichester, John Wiley & Sons.

Williams, S. (2001) *Emotion and Social Theory*, London, Sage.

The values dimension

Adams, R. (2003) *Social Work and Empowerment*, 3rd edn, Basingstoke, Palgrave Macmillan.

Dawson, A. and Butler, I. (2003) 'The Morally Active Manager', in Henderson and Atkinson (2003).

Dean, H. (ed.) (2004) *The Ethics of Welfare: Human Rights, Dependency and Responsibility*, Bristol, The Policy Press.

Griseri, P. (1998) *Managing Values: Ethical Change in Organisations*, Basingstoke, Macmillan.

Hamer, M. (2006) *The Barefoot Helper: Mindfulness and Creativity in Social Work and the Helping Professions*, Lyme Regis, Russell House Publishing.

Hugman, R. (2005) *New Approaches in Ethics for the Caring Professions*, Basingstoke, Palgrave Macmillan.

Kallen, E. (2004) *Social Inequality and Social Justice,* Basingstoke, Palgrave Macmillan.

Moss, B. (2005) *Religion and Spirituality*, Lyme Regis, Russell House Publishing.

Moss, B. (2007) *Values*, Lyme Regis, Russell House Publishing.

Thompson, N. (2003) *Promoting Equality: Challenging Discrimination and Oppression,* 2nd edn, Basingstoke, Palgrave Macmillan.

Thompson, N. (2005) *Understanding Social Work,* 2nd edn, Basingstoke, Palgrave Macmillan – see Chapter 5.

Thompson, N. (2006) *Anti-Discriminatory Practice,* 4th edn, Basingstoke, Palgrave Macmillan.

Thompson, N. (2006) *Promoting Workplace Learning,* Bristol, The Policy Press – see Chapter 2.

Self-management skills

Honey, P. (2003) *How to Become a More Effective Learner,* Maidenhead, Peter Honey Publications.

Honey, P. (2007) *Continuing Personal Development,* Maidenhead, Peter Honey Publications.

Jasper, M. (2003) *Beginning Reflective Practice,* Cheltenham, Nelson Thornes.

Thompson, N. (2002) *People Skills,* 2nd edn, Basingstoke, Palgrave Macmillan.

Thompson, N. (2006) *People Problems,* Basingstoke, Palgrave Macmillan.

Supervision and mentoring

Clutterbuck, D. (1998) *Learning Alliances: Tapping into Talent,* London, CIPD.

Clutterbuck, D. (2001) *Everyone Needs a Mentor: Fostering Talent at Work,* 3rd edn, London, CIPD.

Doel, M. and Shardlow, S.M. (2005) *Modern Social Work Practice: Teaching and Learning In Practice Settings,* Aldershot, Ashgate.

Ghaye, T. and Lillyman, S. (eds) (2000) *Effective Clinical Supervision: The Role of Reflection,* Wiltshire, Quay Books.

Hawkins, P. and Shohet, R. (2001) *Supervision in the Helping Professions,* 2nd edn, Buckingham, Open University Press.

Hughes, L. and Pengelly, P. (eds) (1997) *Staff Supervision in a Turbulent Environment: Managing Process and Task in Front Line Services,* London, Jessica Kingsley.

Jones, M. (2004) 'Supervision, Learning and Transformative Practices', in Gould and Baldwin (2004).

Morrison, T. (2000) *Supervision: An Action Learning Approach,* 2nd edn, Brighton, Pavilion.

Perlmutter, F. D., Bailey, D. and Netting, F. E. (2001) *Managing Human Resources in the Human Services: Supervisory Challenges,* Oxford, Oxford University Press.

Rolfe, G., Freshwater, D. and Jasper, M. (2001) *Critical Reflection for Nursing and the Helping Professions,* Basingstoke, Palgrave Macmillan – see Chapters 4 and 5.

Thompson, N. (2006) *Promoting Workplace Learning,* Bristol, The Policy Press – see Chapter 4.

Learning and development

Clarke, A. (2001) *Learning Organisations: What they Are and How to Become One*, Leicester, National Organisation for Adult Learning.

Cottrell, S. (2005) *Critical Thinking Skills: Developing Effective Analysis and Argument*, Basingstoke, Palgrave Macmillan.

Doel, M., Sawdon, C. and Morrison, D. (2002) *Learning, Practice and Assessment: Signposting the Portfolio*, London, Jessica Kingsley.

Doel, M. (2005) *New Approaches in Practice Learning*, London, Skills for Care.

Fook, J., Ryan, M. and Hawkins, L. (2000) *Professional Expertise: Practice, Theory and Education for Working in Uncertainty*, London, Whiting & Birch.

Ghaye, T. and Lillyman, S. (2006) *Learning Journals and Critical Incidents: Reflective Practice for Health Care Professionals*, 2nd edn, London, Quay Books.

Gibbs, G. (1988) *Learning by Doing: A Guide to Teaching and Learning Methods*, London, Further Education Unit.

Honey, P. (2003) *How to Become an Effective Learner*, Maidenhead, Peter Honey Publications.

Moon, J. A. (1999) *Reflection in Learning and Professional Development*, Abingdon, Routledge Falmer.

Horwarth, J. and Morrison, T. (1999) *Effective Staff Training in Social Care: From Theory to Practice*, London, Routledge.

Osterman, K. F. and Kottkamp, R.B. (2004) *Reflective Practice for Educators, Professional Development to Improve Student Learning*, 2nd edn, London, Sage

Thompson, N. (2006) *Promoting Workplace Learning*, Bristol, The Policy Press.

Waldman, J. (1999) *Help Yourself to Learning at Work*, Lyme Regis, Russell House Publishing.

Tools and strategies for promoting reflective practice

Berne, E. (1961) *Transactional Analysis in Psychotherapy*, New York, Grove Press.

Berne, E. (1964) *Games People Play*, Harmondsworth, Penguin.

Buzan, T. and Buzan, B. (2003) *The Mind Map Book*, 2nd edn, London, BBC Worldwide.

Doel, M. and Shardlow, S.M. (2005) *Modern Social Work Practice: Teaching and Learning in Practice Settings*, Aldershot, Ashgate.

Fook, J., Ryan, M. and Hawkins, L. (2000) *Professional Expertise: Practice, Theory and Education for Working in Uncertainty*, London, Whiting & Birch.

Ghaye, T. and Lillyman, S. (2006) *Learning Journals and Critical Incidents: Reflective Practice for Health Care Professionals*, London, Quay Books.

Gould, N. and Baldwin, M. (eds) (2004) *Social Work, Critical Reflection and the Learning Organization*, Aldershot, Ashgate.

Harris, T. (1973) *I'm OK – You're OK*, London, Pan.

Moon, J. A. (1999) *Reflection in Learning and Professional Development*, Abingdon, Routledge Falmer.

Pitman, E. (1983) *Transactional Analysis for Social Workers*, London, Routledge & Kegan Paul.

Thompson, N. (2006) *People Problems*, Basingstoke, Palgrave Macmillan.

Recording reflection

Bolton, G. (2005) *Reflective Practice: Writing and Professional Development*, 2nd edn, London, Sage.

Ghaye, T. and Lillyman, S. (2006) *Learning Journals and Critical Incidents: Reflective Practice for Health Care Professionals*, London, Quay Books.

Jasper, M. (2003) *Beginning Reflective Practice*, Cheltenham, Nelson Thornes.

Jasper, M. (2004) 'Using Journals and Diaries within Reflective Practice', in Bulman and Schutz (2004).

Moon, J.A. (1999) *Reflection in Learning and Professional Development*, Abingdon, Routledge Falmer.

Rolfe, G., Freshwater, D. and Jasper, M. (2001) *Critical Reflection for Nursing and the Helping Profession*, Basingstoke, Palgrave Macmillan – see Chapter 3.

Assessing reflection

Bolton, G. (2005) *Reflective Practice: Writing and Professional Development*, 2nd edn, London, Sage.

Doel, M., Sawdon, C. and Morrison, D. (2002) *Learning, Practice and Assessment: Signposting the Portfolio*, London, Jessica Kingsley.

Schutz, S, Angrove, C. and Sharp, P. (2004) 'Assessing and Evaluating Reflection', in Bulman and Schutz (2004).

JOURNALS

Active Learning in Higher Education
www.sagepub.co.uk/journalsSearch.nav?_requestid=29669

British Journal of Nursing
www.britishjournalofnursing.com

Journal of Advanced Nursing
www.journalofadvancednursing.com

Journal of Practice Teaching in Health and Social Work
www.whitingbirch.net/ip002.shtml

Learning in Health and Social Care
http://www.blackwellpublishing.com/journal.asp?ref=1473-6853&site=1

Nurse Education Today
http://intl.elsevierhealth.com/journals/nedt/

Nurse Researcher
http://www.nursing-standard.co.uk/nurseresearcher/

Research on Social Work Practice
http://rsw.sagepub.com/

Social Work Education
http://www.tandf.co.uk/journals/titles/02615479.asp

Reflective Practice
http://www.gbhap.com/journals/titles/14623943.asp

ORGANIZATIONS AND WEBSITES

Economic and Social Research Council	www.esrc.ac.uk
Higher Education Academy	www.heacademy.ac.uk
Institute for Reflective Practice	www.reflectivepractices.co.uk
Intute	www.intute.ac.uk
Joseph Rowntree Foundation	www.jrf.org.uk
Making Practice-Based Learning Work	www.practicebasedlearning.org/
National Institute of Adult and Continuing Education	www.niace.org.uk
Research in Practice	www.rip.org.uk
Research in Practice for Adults	www.dartington.org/social-justice
Social Care Institute of Excellence	www.scie.org.uk
SWAP (Social Policy and Social Work)	www.swap.ac.uk

References

Allen, D. G., Bowers, B. and Diekelmann, N. (1989) 'Writing to Learn: A Reconceptualization of Thinking and Writing in the Nursing Curriculum,' *Journal of Nursing Education*, 28(1).

Argyris, C. and Schön, D. (1978) *Organizational Learning: A Theory of Action Perspective*, Reading, MA, Addison-Wesley.

Atkins, S. (2004) 'Developing Underlying Skills in the Move Towards Reflective Practice', in Bulman and Schutz (2004).

Baldwin, M. (2004) 'Critical Reflection: Oportunities and Threats to Professional Learning and Service Development in Social Work Organizations', in Gould and Baldwin (2004).

Bates, J. (2004) 'Promoting Learning Through Reflective Practice', *British Journal of Occupational Learning*, 2(2), pp. 21–32.

Bandman, E. L. and Bandman, B. (1995) *Critical Thinking in Nursing*, 2nd edn, Norwalk, CT, Appleton and Lange.

Bateson, G. (1973) *Steps to an Ecology of Mind: Collected Essays in Anthropology, Psychiatry, Evolution and Epistemology*, St Albans, Paladin.

Benner, P., Hooper-Kyriakidis, P. and Stannard, D. (1999) *Clinical Wisdom and Interventions in Critical Care: A Thinking-in-Action Approach*, Philadelphia, PA, Saunders.

Benner, P., Tanner, C. and Chesla, C. (eds) (1996) *Expertise in Nursing Practice: Caring, Clinical Judgement and Ethics*, New York, Springer.

Borton, T. (1970) *Reach, Touch and Teach*, London, Hutchinson.

Boud, D. and Walker, D. (1990) 'Making the Most of Experience', *Studies in Continuing Education*,12(2).

Brearley, P. (1982) *Risk and Ageing*, London, Routledge.

Brechin, A., Brown, H. and Eby, M. A. (2000a) 'Introduction', in Brechin et al. (2000b).

Brechin, A., Brown, H. and Eby, M. A. (eds) (2000b) *Critical Practice in Health and Social Care*, London, Sage.

Bruner, J. (1996) *The Culture of Education*, Cambridge, MA, Harvard University Press.

Bulman, C. and Schutz, S. (eds) (2004) *Reflective Practice in Nursing*, 3rd edn, Oxford, Blackwell.

Butt, T. (2004), *Understanding People*, Basingstoke, Palgrave Macmillan.

Buzan, T. and Buzan, B. (2003) *The Mind Map Book*, 2nd edn, London, BBC Worldwide.

Calderhead, J. and Gates, P. (eds) (1993) *Conceptualizing Reflection in Teacher Development*, London, Falmer Press.

Christenson, T. (2001) *Wonder and Critical Reflection: An Invitation to Philosophy*, London, Prentice-Hall International.

Clutterbuck, D. (1998) *Learning Alliances: Tapping into Talent*, London, Chartered Institute of Personnel and Development.

Clutterbuck, D. (2001) *Everyone Needs a Mentor: Fostering Talent at Work*, 3rd edn, London, Chartered Institute of Personnel and Development.

Corr, C. A, Nabe, C. M. and Corr, D. M. (2006) *Death and Dying, Life and Living*, 5th edn, Belmont, CA, and London, Thomson Wadsworth.

Cottrell, S. (2005) *Critical Thinking Skills: Developing Effective Analysis and Argument*, Basingstoke, Palgrave Macmillan.

Dewey, J. (1916), *Democracy and Education: An Introduction to the Philosophy of Education*, New York, The Free Press.

Dewey, J. (1933) *How We Think*, Boston, MA, DC Heath.

Dilthey, W. (1988), *Introduction to the Human Sciences: An Attempt to Lay a Foundation for the Study of Society and History*, Oxford, Blackwell.

Doel, M. and Shardlow, S. (2005) *Modern Social Work Practice: Teaching and Learning in Practice Settings*, Aldershot, Ashgate

Doel, M., Sawdon, C. and Morrison, D. (2002) *Learning, Practice and Assessment: Signposting the Portfolio*, London, Jessica Kingsley.

Dolan, P., Canavan, J. and Pinkerton, J. (eds) (2006) *Family Support as Reflective Practice*, London, Jessica Kingsley Publishers.

Doyle, C. (2006) *Working with Abused Children*, 3rd edn, Basingstoke, Palgrave Macmillan.

Dreyfus, H., Dreyfus, S. and Benner, P. (1996) 'Implications of the Phenomenology of Expertise for Teaching and Learning Everyday Skillful Ethical Comportment', in Benner, Tanner and Chesla (1996).

Fook, J. (2002) *Social Work: Critical Theory and Practice*, London, Sage.

Fook, J. (2004) 'Critical Reflection and Organizational Learning and Change: A Case Study', in Gould and Baldwin (2004).

Fook, J. and Askeland, G. A. (2006) 'The "Critical" in Critical Reflection', in White et al. (2006).

Freire, P. (1972) *Pedagogy of the Oppressed*, Harmondsworth, Penguin.

Gambrill, E. (1997) *Social Work Practice: A Critical Thinker's Guide*, Oxford, Oxford University Press.

Gardner, F., Fook, J. and White, S. (2006) 'Critical Reflection: Possibilities for Developing Effectiveness in Conditions of Uncertainty', in White et al. (2006).

Ghaye, T. and Lillyman, S. (2006) *Learning Journals and Critical Incidents: Reflective Practice for Health Care Professionals*, 2nd edn, London, Quay Books.

Gilbert, P. (2004) 'It's Humanity, Stoopid!', Inaugural Professorial Lecture, Staffordshire University, 29 September.

Goffman, E. (1971) *The Presentation of Self in Everyday Life*, Harmondsworth, Penguin.

Gordon, S. (1990) 'Social Structural Effects on Emotions', in Kemper (1990).

Gould, N. (1996) 'Introduction: Social Work Education and the "Crisis of the Professions"', in Gould and Taylor (1996).

Gould, N. and Baldwin, M. (eds) (2004) *Social Work, Critical Reflection and the Learning Organization*, Aldershot, Ashgate.

Gould, N. and Taylor, I. (eds) (1996) *Reflective Learning for Social Work*, Aldershot, Arena.

Griseri, P. (1998) *Managing Values: Ethical Change in Organisations*, Basingstoke, Macmillan – now Palgrave Macmillan.

Hamer, M. (2006) *The Barefoot Helper: Mindfulness and Creativity in Social Work and the Helping Professions*, Lyme Regis, Russell House Publishing.

Harris, A. (1996) 'Learning from Experience and Reflection in Social Work Education', in Gould and Taylor (1996).

Heller, E. (1988) *The Importance of Nietzsche: Ten Essays*, Chicago and London, The University of Chicago Press.

Henderson, J. and Atkinson, D. (eds) (2003) *Managing Care in Context*, London, Routledge.

Hinchcliff, S. M., Norman, S .E. and Schober, J. (eds) (1993) *Nursing Practice and Health Care*, 2nd edn, London, Edward Arnold.

Honey, P. (2003) *How to Become an Effective Learner*, Maidenhead, Peter Honey Publications

Hopkins, J. (1986) *Caseworker*, Birmingham, Pepar Publications.

Hyland, A. (ed.) (2004) *University College Cork as a Learning Organisation*, Cork, University College Cork.

Jasper, M. (2004) 'Using Journals and Diaries within Reflective Practice', in Bulman and Schutz (2004).

Karvinen-Niinikoski, S. (2004) 'Social Work Supervision: Contributing to Innovative Knowledge Development Production and Open Expertise', in Gould and Baldwin (2004).

Katz, J. (1978) *White Awareness: Handbook for Anti-Racist Training*, Norman, OK, University of Oklahoma Press.

Kemper, T. (ed.) (1990) *Research Agendas in the Sociology of the Emotions*, New York, State University of New York Press.

Lewin, K. (1947) 'Feedback Problems of Social Diagnosis and Action', *Human Relations*, 1.

Lovelock, R., Lyons, K. and Powell, J. (eds) (2004) *Reflecting on Social Work – Discipline and Profession*, Aldershot, Ashgate.

Lyons, N. (2004) 'The Centrality of Reflective Engagement in Learning and Professional Development: The UCC Experience', in Hyland (2004).

Mabey, C. and Iles, P. (eds) (1994) *Managing Learning*, London, Routledge.

Mezirow, J. (1983) 'Critical Theory of Adult Learning and Education', *Education for Adults*, 1.

Mezirow, J. and associates (1990) *Fostering Critical Reflection in Adulthood*, San Fransisco, CA, Jossey-Bass.

Moon, J.A. (1999) *Reflection in Learning and Professional Development: Theory and Practice*, Abingdon, RoutledgeFalmer.

Morrison, K. (1996) 'Developing Reflective Practice in Higher Degree Students through a Learning Journal', *Studies in Higher Education*, 21(3).

Moss, B. (2005) *Religion and Spirituality*, Lyme Regis, Russell House.

Moss, B. (2007) *Values*, Lyme Regis, Russell House.

Murray, M. and Kujundzic, N. (2005) *Critical Reflection: A Textbook for Critical Thinking*, Montreal and Kingston/ London, McGill-Queen's University Press.

Parton, N. (1998) 'Risk, Advanced Liberalism and Child Welfare: The Need to Rediscover Uncertainty and Ambiguity', *British Journal of Social Work*, 28(1).

Payne, M. (2000) *Anti-Bureaucratic Social Work*, Birmingham, Venture Press.

Proctor, K. (1993 'Tutors' Professional Knowledge of Supervision and the Implications for Supervision Practice', in Calderhead and Gates (1993).

Quinn, F. M. (1998a) 'Reflection and Reflective Practice', in Quinn (1998b).

Quinn, F. M. (ed.) (1998b) *Continuing Professional Development in Nursing*, Cheltenham, Stanley Thornes.

Riches, G. and Dawson, P. (2000) *An Intimate Loneliness: Supporting Bereaved Parents and Siblings*, Buckingham, Open University Press.

Rolfe, G., Freshwater, D. and Jasper, M. (2001) *Critical Reflection for Nursing and the Helping Professions: A User Guide*, Basingstoke, Palgrave Macmillan.

Scheff, T. J. (1997) *Emotions, The Social Bond, and Human Reality: Part/Whole Analysis*, Cambridge, Cambridge University Press.

Schober, J. (1993) 'Frameworks for Nursing Practice', in Hinchcliff et al. (1993).

Schön, D. A. (1983) *The Reflective Practitioner: How Professionals Think in Action*, New York, Basic Books.

Senge, P. M. (1994) 'The Leader's New Work: Building Learning Organizations', in Mabey and Iles (1994).

Smyth, J. (1989) 'Developing and Sustaining Critical Reflection in Teacher Education', *Journal of Teacher Education*, 40(2).

Taylor, B. J. (2006) *Reflective Practice: A Guide for Nurses and Midwives*, 2nd edn, Maidenhead, Open University Press/McGraw-Hill Education

Taylor, C. and White, S. (2000) *Practising Reflexivity in Health and Welfare: Making Knowledge*, Buckingham, Open University Press.

Thompson, N. (2000) *Theory and Practice in the Human Services*, 2nd edn, Buckingham, Open University Press.

Thompson, N. (2002) *People Skills*, 2nd edn, Basingstoke, Palgrave Macmillan.

Thompson, N. (2003) *Communication and Language: A Handbook of Theory and Practice*, Basingstoke, Palgrave Macmillan.

Thompson, N. (2005) *Understanding Social Work*, 2nd edn, Basingstoke, Palgrave Macmillan

Thompson, N. (2006a) *Promoting Workplace Learning*, Bristol, The Policy Press.

Thompson, N. (2006b) *People Problems*, Basingstoke, Palgrave Macmillan.

Thompson, N. (2007) *Power and Empowerment*, Lyme Regis, Russell House Publishing.

Warren, M. P. (2006) *From Trauma to Transformation*, Carmarthen, Crown House.

Wheen, F. (2000) *Karl Marx*, London, 4th Estate.

White, S., Fook, J. and Gardner, F. (eds) (2006) *Critical Reflection in Health and Social Care*, Maidenhead, Open University Press/McGraw-Hill Education.

Williams, S. (2001) *Emotion and Social Theory: Corporeal Reflections on the (Ir)rational*, London, Sage.

Index

LIBRARY, UNIVERSITY OF CHESTEF

LIBRARY, UNIVERSITY OF CHESTER